Cognitive Set Theory

Alec Mead Rogers

Cognitive Set Theory

Alec Mead Rogers

http://www.cognitivesettheory.com

ArborRhythms
Newton, MA

Publication date 2012-04-27

Printed in the United States of America.

ISBN: 978-0-98303-760-6

Library of Congress Control Number: 2010919532

Dedication

This book is dedicated to all the people with whom I ever ate lunch, many of whom were forced to discuss the nature of existence of the salt and pepper shakers.

Also, I would like to thank the salt and pepper shakers: I never doubted you for an instant.

Table of Contents

List of Figures

List of Tables

List of Equations

Introduction

What is this thing?

This book is a study of unity, multiplicity, and references. It examines the world, our experience of it, and our thought about it, while focusing on the relation of the part to the whole. It is about our concepts: how they are formed, how they are shaped by the world, and how they in turn shape the world. It is mildly ironic to examine reality by first taking it apart and then putting it back together: perhaps that is my karma as an engineer.

This book is also a study of three general types of things: everything, something, and nothing. These things are examined from three points of view: the physical, the subjective, and the conceptual. One of the main goals of this book is to develop a somewhat formal language for cognition: to do so, it relies heavily on the sciences of set theory and mereology.

This book takes primarily a holistic, or nondualistic, perspective: in other words, it begins by examining *everything*. It then proceeds to examine *something*, which is formed by dividing *everything*. This division is often carried out hierarchically: parts themselves are subdivided, thereby forming a structure that resembles a tree. This nondualistic orientation holds that the whole comes before (or is ontologically prior to) its parts. Last but not least, *nothing* is discussed, in no small part because it nicely complements the discussion of everything. Nothing is also significant in virtue of being a reference: references are those things which allow us to build concepts out of smaller constituents, and whose manipulation is called thought.

Why did I write this thing? I wrote this book in order to share several simple ideas. These ideas pertain to the relations between parts, wholes, and references, which are familiar subjects to all of us. But despite their frequent use, these subjects receive relatively little attention. This book attempts to remedy that situation: it strives to lay a broad foundation for thinking about parts, wholes, and references from a number of different points of view.[1]

Why should you read this thing? Perhaps you have some interest in the organization and operational principles of our material and mental lives. Perhaps you have an affinity for a "holistic" or "nondualistic" approach, and you would like to understand more about the relationship of parts to wholes and how that influences, and is influenced by, cognition. You might also be interested in understanding the parallels between set theory and cognition.

Although the subject matter of this book is wide-ranging, most of it is related to parts, wholes, references as these things relate to the structures behind language and cognition. The title is indicative of this subject matter: cognition (psychology) and set theory (mathematics) are interwoven. Since the technical details of this endeavor are of interest only to a small portion of readers, the first several parts of this book are relatively informal; the formal details are presented in the last part of this book.

What is the structure of this thing? This book is written in four parts.

The first part of this book is an introduction to *things*. Things are split into three general types: everythings, somethings, and nothings. This three-part division of things is based on the space which things occupy; a thing is defined in terms of its spatial boundaries.

Space, in the sense that term is used in this book, is not limited to a single physical (three-dimensional) space: it may be multidimensional (i.e. one which may have an arbitrary number of dimensions, and which is sometimes called N-space) or even a conceptual space. The dimensionality of the space is assumed to be equivalent to the objects in it: for example, four-dimensional space is necessary to contain four-dimensional things. As an example, a four-dimensional thing could be a three-dimensional thing that occupies a temporal extent (i.e. a single, continuing three-dimensional thing may be considered to be a four-dimensional thing).[2]

The second and third parts of this book discuss universes and several primary relations between these universes, respectively. The universes are created by successively partitioning the physical universe. First, the physical universe is divided into two parts, the subjective and the objective. The subjective part is further divided into perceptual and conceptual parts. In this way, three things are created, which are called universes. The reason for partitioning everything in this way, as opposed to some other, is that the resulting parts are composed of *references*: the conceptual universe refers to the subjective universe, which in turn refers to the physical universe.

References form the basis of universes: the division between one universe and another similarly divides the referrers from the referents. For example, the subjective universe contains references to the objective universe. From the subjective point of view, these references are responsible for perception. From the objective point of view, references are physical things just like any other. This dual characteristic of references is what makes them so special, and what makes the boundaries between universes composed of references so odd.

The fourth and final part of this book is aimed at technically-oriented readers: it offers a more formal summary of most topics discussed in the book.[3] Finally, the various appendices should be treated as reference material for the rest of the book: it is advisable to at least skim that section first.

Notes

[1] I have a passion for mathematics, philosophy, and psychology, which I anticipate many readers will share. Despite my passion, I sometimes find the presentation of these subjects somewhat impenetrable. Therefore, a primary aim of this book is to make mathematics relevant, philosophy unconvoluted, and psychology beautiful.

[2] For some readers, it may clarify things to think in terms of "events" and "spacetime" instead of in terms of "things" and "space", since the former terms connote having more than three dimensions. However, the former terms imply four-dimensional physical entities: in the general case, being limited to either four dimensions or the physical world is undesirable (since this might exclude such things as perceptual spaces).

[3] The summary of the book does not contain a summary of the entire book, but only a summary of the parts of the book that have been written before the summary.

Part I: Things

In a general sense, there are three types of objects: everythings, somethings, and nothings. In a universe, there can exist only one everything, many somethings, and exactly zero nothings.

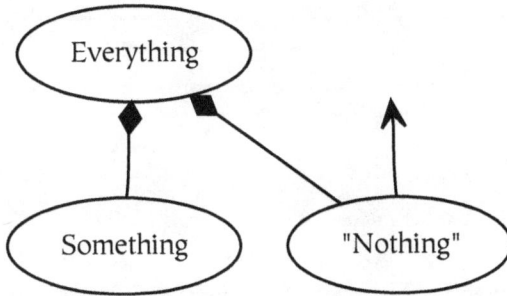

Chapter 1: Everything

Everything means *every thing*, taken together. Although it may be conceptualized as a single unit, it is best to regard everything as something which is neither singular nor plural (because the concept of singularity requires the concept of plurality).

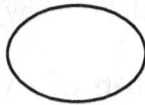

We have depicted everything in the diagram above. We have not bothered to label it, because there is nothing from which to distinguish it. We have drawn a boundary around it to help to visualize it, but this is somewhat mistaken since everything is unbounded: the boundary is not present if everything is recognized.

1.1: The Whole

Everything cannot be defined.

Everything cannot be defined. It is impossible to say what it is, and it is impossible to say what it is not. Everything is a whole which initially is without parts and without the lack of parts. Despite the fact that it serves as the starting point, it is that thing which (at least from one point of view) cannot be transcended.

A Definition of Everything

Everything occupies every position in all dimensions which are attributed to it.

It is difficult to define everything, since there is nothing to which it can be compared (other than itself). Definitions are always given in terms of other things, so it is impossible to define a thing for which there is no other thing. There is no other when it comes to "the one without a second".

This book begins with everything, which seems appropriate given that our mental worlds begin in the same way. Conceptually, it is difficult to understand everything. Everything should not be understood as *many things taken together* or as a *single whole*; both of these concepts are limiting, and they cannot be applied to everything without thereby restricting its scope to some portion of itself. Everything should not be understood as "every object at a single instant in time", but as everything-everywhere *and* everything-everywhen. In this sense everything can be considered an event, because it has both a spatial and a temporal extent.[1] Again, the extension of the word "everything" in the world (i.e. the object that the word refers to) has no thing outside of it. If one believes in multiple universes, then these multiple universes should also be included in the concept of everything.

Although it is somewhat mistaken to make a characteristic (or attributive) statement about everything, it may help to consider everything as "undifferentiated" to counter previous misconceptions. For example, this might help to correct the points of view that everything is either a compound entity (one which is made up of parts), or a simple entity (which consists of only one part). However, knowing what it is to be undifferentiated requires knowing what it is to be differentiated; since "everything" is the first concept that we wish to introduce, there is no differentiated thing with which to contrast it. From a subjective point of view, everything exists prior to the properties used to categorize it: because these properties serve to discriminate one thing from another, it is impossible to define any properties on the basis of only one thing.

In both the case where everything is considered as a single entity and where it is considered to be multiple entities, the thing or things referred to are the same in that they have the same spatiotemporal extent. In this case, it is the decomposition (or composition) of everything that is different. From a nominalist point of view, it is the *consideration* of everything that makes it one thing or another: everything remains undifferentiated, independent of our consideration of it. [2]

The fact that everything might be considered to be both one thing and many things highlights two different notions of identity: one which is evaluated spatially, and one which is evaluated in language (between references). Things which occupy the same space (and the same time) are identical, so from one point of view, there is no difference between one thing and many things (as long as they occupy the same space). From another point of view, two things are not the same as one thing in that the symbols which reference those things are not identical. For example, "an apple" is materially (spatially) equivalent to its "seeds, skin, stem and fruit", although these things have different criteria for identity on a conceptual (descriptive) level. The "everything" being described here is that which is materially equivalent to all of its parts (no matter how, or even if, it is decomposed).

Everything is ineffable. Even the morphological parts of the term "everything" indicate that to describe everything, it is broken into parts ("things") and then collected together again ("every"). Spatial metaphors are used to describe it, although this may be overly restrictive, since most spatial metaphors are typically limited to three dimensions. A more nominalistic stance would hold that everything has as many dimensions *as are necessary* for a given description. More precisely, for every dimension which space possesses, *everything* occupies every part of that dimension. This description covers the rather interesting case in which the universe itself does not have a particular dimensionality in isolation from the language used to describe it. [3]

The Properties of Everything

Everything neither has properties nor has no properties.

Everything cannot be called large, but neither can it be called small. Likewise, everything is neither singular nor plural. It is not the case that everything has properties.

However, neither is it the case that everything has no properties. The combination of these statements is somewhat of a puzzle, since most things either have a property or do not have that property. However, if the nature of words is relativistic, then there is no sense to be made of something which has no comparator; and that is exactly how everything is defined. Everything cannot be compared to something, since there is no something other than everything: to compare something to itself is tautologous. Conceptually, since no relative judgment is possible, no judgment whatsoever is possible: conceptual judgment is inherently relative.

Perhaps calling a thing both good and bad is an attempt to make the ineffable, effable; perhaps the best description of the ineffable characterizes it with every possible term, as well as the opposite of that term (e.g. everything is both good and bad). A complementary attempt to describe everything utilizes the negation of both terms (e.g. everything is neither good nor bad). While it is incorrect to say anything about everything because of the potential for misunderstanding, this book follows the latter convention: with respect to a property P_x, "everything is not P_x" *and* "everything is not not-P_x" (this implies that "not P_x" is what is called a *non-affirming* negative).

It is important to note that in saying that there is no absolute conceptual goodness, we are not advocating any sort of moral relativism. There is certainly such a thing as doing good, but it entails a particular perspective: for example, doing good often implies doing good for other people. One might hold certain things to be good in themselves, but there must be bad things to which they are compared. Further, those good things are only good in a particular context. For example, although there may be a sense in which everything is good at a particular time, that is probably relative to a previous time when things were not so good.

Some people might disagree that definitions are inherently relative; they may hold that "good" is an objective characteristic. In other words, an object's goodness does not require comparison with some other object, so this goodness is not relative to something else. Non-relative (objective) goodness, however, is full of contradiction: it is impossible to know what good means anymore if there is no longer any bad. Further, if the concept of "good" is not relative to "bad" (i.e. if the two do not lie on opposite ends of a single continuum), then a single thing could be both good and bad.[4]

Applying a relative term to a wholeness, or something which is not itself a part of something else, poses a paradox. For example, in the introduction to a radio show A Prairie Home Companion, it is said of a town called Lake Woebegone that "... all the children are above average." Although this is a pleasing image, it is not logically possible. Being above average is clearly relativistic, so not everybody can be above average; in order for someone to be above average, someone else must be below average. Finding a comparator in this case is not a problem: the people of Lake Woebegone are smarter than the people of Shelbyville. For everyone to be above average, however, there is a problem: if the population referred to by "all the children" is the same population from which the average is calculated, somebody must have a below-average child (apologies to the relevant mommies and daddies).

There is a mismatch between the thing *everything* and the terms used to describe it: *everything* is absolute, but terminology is relativistic. Conventionally, one might say that everything has this or that property, but this entails comparing one concept of the world with another, and this latter comparison says more about concepts then it does about the world.

1.2: Universes

Universes are everything from a particular point of view.

This book describes several universes. Since the term *universe* is generally construed to be all-inclusive, it may seem counterintuitive to have more than one of them. On the one hand, the physical universe contains all of the other universes as parts. When referring to this all-inclusive universe, it is known as *the* universe. However, there are other entities which are in some sense unbounded, in light of which they will also be called universes. It is of course odd to have multiple unbounded entities, especially if some are parts of another, so the existence of multiple unbounded entities must be further elaborated.

To reiterate, *the* universe is that which contains absolutely everything: in this absolute sense, there can clearly be only one universe (which is why the definite article is emphasized in this context). However, the universe as seen from a particular reference point is also a universe: it is a universe from the subjective point of view (or point of reference). These subjective universes, based on particular points of view, are composed of references to the containing universe.

Subjective universes exist within the universe, as well as being universes in their own right. Just as a reference is itself a thing and a reference to a thing, so a universe which consists of references is both a referential universe and contained in the universe (to which its references refer). To use a more concrete example: spoken words may stand for something else, but they are also themselves sounds. So the universe of spoken words is both contained in the universe of sounds, and it is a universe of its own (when the words are understood as references). When a given referential universe is viewed in relationship to *the* universe, it is seen to be a part of it: in that larger context (or from that larger perspective), these referential universes are merely parts. On the other hand, when they are viewed from their own perspective, they operate *as* the entire universe, in the sense that nothing exists outside of them *from that perspective*.

To borrow an example from a later section of this book, the subjective universe is everything that an individual can perceive. Everything, from a subjective point of view, is the entire field of perception. Although the subjective universe can be restricted by attention, which limits what is perceived (or conceived), a given perceiver will never perceive outside of their perceptual universe. In this sense, it is complete: it is a whole, or a totality. From the subjective perspective, references to physical things are everything that exists: therefore, subjective experience forms a universe. Similarly, although concepts may be restricted to some *domain of discourse*, concepts also form a universe. The conceptual mind lives in a universe of concepts, in that nothing can be conceived which is not a concept.

To use a more concrete example, our house may be a part of the world which we enter and leave, but if we never leave it, it is our universe. People may come and visit, and tell us of the world outside, and we may form an idea of the world outside, but we still form an idea of the world outside *from within our house*. There is nothing inside of our house which is outside of our house. Universes are like this; it is possible to have references to things outside of a universe from inside of a universe, and many things can be accommodated (referentially) within that universe. From the referential perspective, the set of references is complete, unbounded, and whole. However, from the perspective of the larger container, references are categorically different than the things they point to, and these universes are incomplete, bounded, and merely parts.

To return to the subject of the (physical) universe, it is defined to contain all of the other universes. This containment relationship between the physical and other universes is often taken for granted, but it is not the only possibility. For example, we might believe that the subjective universe contains the physical universe. In other words, our only knowledge of the external world comes through experience with the subjective world, so it is not possible to confirm that there is an objective world independent of the subjective world.[5]

1.3: The Integrity of Wholes

Wholes, as opposed to collections of parts, are united.

What is it to be a whole? For a thing to be a whole means that it is united: a single thing. Although it may be composed of other things, and it may in turn compose other things, there is some integral quality to it.

For a thing to be an integrated whole also seems to imply that there is something else with which it can be differentiated. Wholeness is the result of a boundary: it makes everything inside the boundary the same thing, and everything outside a different thing. *Everything* is not like this, in that it does not have an inside and an outside (these are qualities only of *something*).

Wholes do not generally overlap one another, although things can be at least partially coextensive with other things (i.e. they can occupy the same space). For example, this coextensiveness is allowed when the material is the same: the top 2/3 of my body is partially coextensive with the bottom 2/3 of my body. In this case, it is not the things that overlap, but the references to them. Overlap is generally not allowed when the material constituting the things is not the same. In fact, it is not even clear what it would mean for different material to occupy the same space, unless one of the things is tangible and the other is some sort of an ethereal, ghost-like thing.[6]

Wholes are said to be greater than the sum of their parts, which is a bit of a puzzling notion. There is at least one way in which it is true, and one in which it is false. On one hand, a whole is not greater than the sum of its parts if we understand identity materially: the material that composes a whole is exactly the material that composes its parts. For example, the material that constitutes the wheels, body, and the rest of a car is equivalent to the material that constitutes the entire car. On the other hand, a whole is greater than the sum of its parts if we consider properties such as the relations between parts to be properties of the whole, and not properties of the parts themselves (e.g. the spatial arrangement of parts). For example, the wheels, body, and the rest of a car are not sufficient to carry you about if they are lying in a heap.

A further claim about what makes wholes more than just the sum of their parts has to do with *emergent properties*. Emergent properties are said to *emerge* only when considering the whole, and are not properties of the parts of that whole. An example of this claim is that simple neuronal elements connected in varying ways leads to a brain: a whole which has properties that are not properties of the individual elements. Whether or not these properties *could* have been predicted based on knowledge of the smaller parts is the subject of some debate. In either case, the behavior of the whole can certainly be quite difficult to predict based on knowledge of the individual elements.[7]

In summary, there is something cohesive about things. Physical things tend to be cohesive in that three-dimensional objects often maintain their (approximate) shape. By contrast, the labels which we apply to these things are even more cohesive: objects are changing all the time, but their names are not.[8] Although using the same word for slightly different objects leads to an economy of expression, it is prudent to ensure that this categorical understanding does not reduce our relationship with reality to one which is exclusively categorical.

Notes

[1]Note that the use of the word "spatial" in this context denotes the three-dimensional (classical) notion of space. More often, the use of the term space in this book should be understood in a mathematical sense, where it may have an arbitrary number of dimensions. In this latter sense, it is often called N-space, where N is the number of dimensions.

[2]The fact that everything is undifferentiated, but our conception of it is differentiated, is somewhat odd since all things (conception included) constitute parts of this everything.

[3]This description is nominalistic in the sense that is not as much of a characteristic statement about everything as it is a conditional statement: there is no commitment to the fact that everything must have (a particular) dimensionality.

[4]It is conceptually meaningless for a thing to be both good and bad at the same time, from the same perspective, using the same criteria for assigning the terms.

[5]The discussion of the way that different universes relate to one another is analogous to the philosophical debate about monism and dualism. This discussion focuses on the relationship between the world of ideas (or perhaps the world of the spirit) and the world of matter. Roughly, dualists believe that both matter and spirit exist, and that they are different; monists believe in the ultimate existence of either only ideas or only matter (these two subgroups are called idealists and materialists, respectively).

[6]We assume that if things do not occupy the same space, then they do not occupy the same space at a small physical scale, either (which rules out mixtures of things).

[7]For a popular example, visit the boids link at http://www.cognitivesettheory.com/links

[8]Thank goodness. I have a problem even with names that are not changing all of the time.

Chapter 2: Something

Something is the result of partitioning a larger thing.

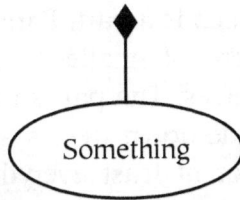

This picture depicts *something*. The attached diamond-headed arrow indicates parthood: something, unless it is everything, is always a part of something else (in this drawing, that larger thing has been omitted).

2.1: Parts

The partition of a thing and the parts of that thing entail one another.

This book begins with everything, and then introduces a partition (or division). This partition entails the creation of at least two other things, each of which is a part. Parts constitute everything, are potentially collections of smaller things, and are of course things in and of themselves. The part structure of things can be represented as an upside-down tree: a single trunk at the top represents everything, or at least everything in the domain of discourse. This tree can be described using the terminology of a family tree: the parent thing gives rise to (and is depicted above) the child things, which are siblings of one another.[1]

Often, something is described in terms of its constituents, the somethings of which it is composed. For example, sets are often defined as collections of elements; cars are often described in terms of their engines, wheels, and so forth. In this book, this bias is countered by emphasizing that things are parts of a larger whole, thereby emphasizing the relationship of a part and its complement. These two descriptions are not incompatible, but they are certainly different; they emphasize different points of view. How a thing is initially defined often emphasizes what is most important about that thing, or at least what about it is most salient. It is also indicative of which concepts arose first in the conceptual universe. The first concepts are often used as the edifice of subsequent concepts, and are essential to the archeology of our conceptual landscape.

The holistic tendency to explain things in terms of their relation to everything contrasts with the reductionistic tendency to explain things in terms of their relation to their smaller constituents. The holistic point of view emphasizes that something is always a part of something larger, with only one exception: everything, which is the singular starting point for all part hierarchies. This everything cannot be explained by holistic theories, just as atoms cannot be explained by reductionistic theories. Despite this holistic emphasis adopted here, it is probably not possible to divide an undifferentiated whole into two parts if there is not *some* difference within its constitutive "stuff". Therefore, the creation of something is collectivizing as well as dichotomizing.

As the epigraph of this section states, "The partition of a thing and the parts of that thing entail one another". This implies both that a partition implies parts and that a part implies a partition. The later fact tends to be overlooked by a reductionistic description of the part: for example, we may describe some part of a thing, but neglect the effect of that description on the counterpart of the described thing. In other words, the fact that *two* things are created by dividing the larger whole sometimes goes unnoticed, despite the fact that it has a number of logical consequences. One way to ameliorate this issue might be to ask "which *boundaries* really exist?" instead of "which *things* really exist?". Although it is a bit of a chicken-and-egg situation, perhaps it is useful to conceive of the division between parts coming before the identification of the parts themselves: the boundary between objects creates the objects.

The following picture illustrates, by means of a dotted line, the things which are implied whenever we talk about "something" (i.e. that something is almost always a part of something larger). This larger thing serves as a context in which something should be understood: the role played by this larger whole is analogous to the *domain of discourse* [Boole]. As it is larger than the thing under consideration, another thing (the copart of the original part) is also implied.

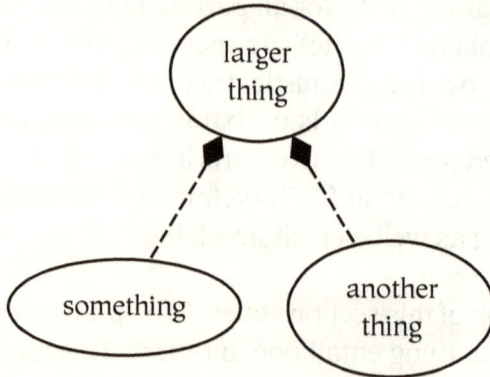

The creation of a partition also implies the creation of a dimension, which is simply an axis along which divisions are possible. In the simple case of a dichotomy, the dimension allows the parent thing to be divided into two children. For example, if an apple can be divided into a stem and a fruit, then this dichotomy implies a dimension along which these parts are divided (although in this case, the dimension is neither linear, nor associated with a well-known name).[2]

Clearly, some divisions have a greater pragmatic value than others; if we are hungry, it makes more sense to identify apples as opposed to red things. However, apart from this pragmatic valuation, are there any qualities of the objects to which we refer that make them more highly qualified as objects, as opposed to other possible objects? In other words, is there any reason to (necessarily) decompose the universe in one way as opposed to another? Although the answer to this question necessarily remains speculative, it seems that everything has the capacity to be divided in numerous different ways (at least conceptually). The basis of this partitioning is a central topic of this book.

To summarize, here is a brief list of the characteristics of somethings (parts) that will be investigated in further detail:

- Parts are created by a division of everything. The divisions are merely decision boundaries, and not necessarily physical boundaries (e.g. a perfectly smooth marble may be conceptually divided into a left and a right half). A collection of one or more boundaries defines a dimension.

- The creation of a part is also the creation of a partition; one of the things created by the partition is the part in question, which is often associated with a label.[3]

- Necessarily, dimensionless entities cannot have parts. Similarly, entities with an associated *proper* (or nontrivial) dimension necessarily have parts.

- Partitions can be repeatedly applied to parts, so that hierarchies of parts are formed (under the assumption of continuity).

- There are many ways to partition something. Hence, a given something may be identified as a part within a larger context, or it may be identified in virtue of the parts that it contains.

- If everything can be divided in arbitrary ways (using various non-unique partitions), it merits investigation why we divide it exactly as we do.

- In addition to being split, parts can also be combined to form new entities. Hence, although parts are the result of partitions, their subsequent recombination allows for the creation of discontiguous entities.[4]

- The partition occurs before the part. As a result, parts and their counterparts have an equal (ontological) footing (even if only one of them is named).

2.2: Atoms

The smallest thing has no parts.

The word "atom", as defined by the early Greek and Indian philosophers who invented the term, means literally uncuttable or indivisible. The atom is therefore the smallest thing, since it has no parts. For a universe to be atomic (i.e. to have parts which are atomic) means that the process of creating parts cannot occur indefinitely: there are small things which cannot be subdivided.

In the physical universe, the name "atom" now represents a particular kind of particle. Unfortunately, that particle was subsequently found to contain parts (atoms have electrons, neutrons, and protons as parts). Oddly enough, the name stuck to the particle, despite the fact that the particle ceased to earn its name. The quest to find increasingly small particles has continued, and today it remains an open question whether the physical universe is atomic or not.

In addition to physical atoms, we may wish to consider *perceptual atoms*. In the perceptual universe, the smallest difference in perception is referred to in psychology as the "just noticeable difference". From a physical point of view, the just noticeable difference may be bounded below by the firing of a single neuron (although there are also numerous chemical changes that are associated with this event). In other words, if we assume that our perception is mediated by the electrical interaction of the neurons in our brains, then the smallest unit of information which we are able to perceive is the firing of a neuron. From a perceptual point of view, however, this neuronal firing is the smallest observable change, so it might be a candidate for the title of "perceptual atom". However, this perceptual atom is so small relative to perception as a whole that perception, even if it is not continuous, is a discrete approximation of continuity.

The determination of whether or not concepts are atomic is complicated because the scientific study of concepts and the conceptual universe is contentious: verbal report of mental states is notoriously unreliable. Hence, in order to measure concepts, we will measure their near analogues, symbols (not the perception of them, but the conception of them). The smallest units of symbolic meaning are morphemes, which in many cases correspond to words (or more technically, lexemes). Morphemes are atomic in that they are not composed of smaller meaningful parts, as with other parts of speech. Although the *representation* of a concept is not atomic (it consists of letters or sounds and has a distributed representation in the brain), and the *object referenced* by a concept may or may not be atomic, is a central thesis of this book that concepts are atomic.

Parts of Reduced Dimensionality

Something cannot have a dimensionality less than its parent thing; it occupies a nonzero interval on every dimension which the parent occupies.

Can something have a dimensionality less than the whole of which it is a part? Although one could imagine something that occupied an arbitrarily small extent along one of the dimensions of the parent thing, to posit that something has *no* extent along one of its dimensions leads to a large number of Zeno-like paradoxes.

One of the older of a number of conundrums related to this topic asks how many points exist on a line (where points are assumed to be zero-dimensional things and lines are assumed to be one-dimensional things). Although one branch of modern mathematics provides a ready answer, it is debatable whether this answer is truly substantive. In particular, although we have named the answer, it may not be that we have actually defined the answer in meaningful terms. The name given to the answer, an "uncountable infinity of points", is not a number like other numbers. For example, it does not grow when other numbers are added to it. In some sense, then, it is not a number at all, at least in the sense of the original question.

A similar problem is posed by understanding *space* as composed of zero-dimensional points. Maintaining that volumes are composed of points corresponds to the mathematical notion of point sets. Point sets assume that things are composed of points, or atoms which are of a lower dimensionality than the larger whole which they occupy. Unfortunately, this understanding forces points that lie *on the boundary* between one object and another to be associated with either one object or the other. This poses problems because the boundaries of objects (and hence the objects themselves) become characteristically different: the object possessing this boundary is said to be "closed", and the object lacking this boundary is said to be "open". One of the many problems which result from this view is that two closed objects cannot touch each other, since between any two points are an infinite number of other points.[5]

This does not mean that all talk of points, lines, and other such objects is discounted, but it does mean that none of their dimensions will be allowed to have an extent of zero. In other words, points are taken to correspond to atoms whose extent is (only) arbitrarily small: perhaps infinitesimal, but still nonzero. Boundaries, on the other hand, are free to have a lower dimensionality, since they do not exist as parts in the space that they divide.

2.3: Properties

The properties of something may be extrinsic or intrinsic. All objects have extrinsic properties except everything, and all objects have intrinsic properties except atoms.

There are several different ways to say what an apple is, or to give a description of it. One alternative is to define it functionally:

it is something to eat, or something that grows on trees. These are extrinsic properties of an apple, because they depend on the apple's relationship with other things. The apple can also be defined intrinsically, by defining some characteristic property of apple-matter. That property is attributed to the apple itself; it is relatively independent of the apple's relationship with other things.

The distinction between intrinsic and extrinsic properties is important to keep in mind when describing the conditions for identity between two objects. Twins, for example, may be intrinsically identical if they have the same physical appearance and parts (under the assumption that different material of the same type is identical). They are not extrinsically identical, however: at the very least, their spatial positions are distinguishable.

A close approximation of this distinction between intrinsic/ extrinsic properties is the distinction between interior/exterior properties.[6] For example, a property of apples such as "being eaten by people" is an extrinsic property. Properties such as "being eaten by worms" are also probably extrinsic properties, even if the worm is *inside* of the apple (which makes it clear that the matter is not always clear-cut). One might argue that the boundaries of the apple do not include the worm; in any case, the essential piece of information that makes a property extrinsic is its dependence on some other thing.

Given the relatively holistic presentation in this book, extrinsic properties are emphasized. A thing has extrinsic properties in virtue of its relation to other things. The intrinsic properties of a thing, therefore, can be defined as the extrinsic properties of that thing's parts. Accordingly, it is clear that a thing which is not a part of something else does not have extrinsic properties, and a thing with no parts does not have intrinsic properties. The two things satisfying these criteria are known as the universe and the atom, respectively. In terms of location (instead of properties), since there are no objects outside of the universe, there are no objects in terms of which to define it: hence, it cannot have an extrinsic definition. At the other end of the continuum of size is the atom: a thing with no parts cannot have an extrinsic definition between its parts, therefore it does not have an intrinsic definition.[7]

Intrinsic Properties

Intrinsic properties characterize the parts of a thing.

Intrinsic properties describe or define an object in terms of its parts. This method of definition is exploited by reductionism. For example, to understand the behavior of an individual reduces to the sciences of physiology and psychology (which describe the activities of the brain). Psychological understanding reduces to the science of biology, which studies the activities of the neurons that constitute the brain. Biology, in turn, reduces to chemistry or physics, which studies the molecules that make up the neurons.

Ultimately, this reduction results in a very detailed explanation, but not necessarily an increase of explanatory power. The big is not *caused* by the small, just as the parts are not caused by the whole. They are simply different levels of description, both of which are a valid description of reality (albeit descriptions of reality that deal with differently sized or shaped parts). While a description that uses small parts may be more detailed, it is also more complicated. So, while it is possible to describe a person by using a physical description that corresponds to the movement of their molecular parts, it is not necessarily of great benefit. In fact, the description of an individual in terms of various neurotransmitters might be substantially less useful than a physiological description, since we know how to affect physiological change more easily (which of course has an effect on chemicals in the brain).

Extrinsic Properties

Extrinsic properties characterize the whole of which a thing is a part.

Extrinsic properties can be investigated in the linguistic domain by examining the meanings of words (or more specifically, morphemes, lexemes, and phrases). The symbolic equivalent of the extrinsic definition of an object is the definition of one symbol (or phrase) using other symbols. The intrinsic description of the corresponding concept would be an analysis of its constituent words or morphemes. Both of these definitions occur in most dictionaries, which provide both the etymology of a word and the definition of that word using other words.

An interesting test for the extrinsic identity of symbols is known as linguistic substitutability. If two different words or phrases are able to be used in the same context (i.e. the same position in a given sentence), then they are linguistically substitutable, which most often implies that they are of the same type, or that they can play the same role. For example, "ball" and "boy" are substitutable in the following sentences (in that they do not change the meaning of the larger context), but "bucket" is not:

1. Kick the ball.

2. Kick the boy.

3. Kick the bucket. (*understood as a synonym for "to die"*)

The last example is interesting because it demonstrates that "bucket" in this context is not a semantically complete thing. The idiomatic expression "kick the bucket" means to die, which is not a compound that involves the meaning of the word "bucket". The semantics of "bucket" is irrelevant in this context: the word "bucket" acts like a phoneme instead of a morpheme.

The context of a word can determine one of several definitions of that word. More precisely, the single word is called a *homonym*, and the multiple words (i.e. those with different meanings) are called *lexemes*. To illustrate this, the preceding examples can be altered as follows:

1. We had a ball.

2. We had a boy.

3. We had a bucket.

"Having a ball" might connote either having a fun time or having a round toy in this context, which illustrates that the homonym "ball" contains at least two lexemes. In the second phrase, having a boy probably connotes that we have given birth to a child, which illustrates that the verb "to have" is a homonym. Finally, the word "bucket" in this context, as opposed to its context in the previous example, is once again a complete noun, meaningful on its own (or at least meaningful to a greater degree).

There are at least two different ways to understand homonyms. Under one understanding, a single word may contain multiple definitions, each of which is complete. Under another, the single word contains an *incomplete* definition, which can only be completed in context. And just as the definition of a word may be intrinsic or extrinsic, there are numerous things which are similarly incomplete or ambiguous without a larger (clarifying) context.

Relativistic Properties

Properties characterize the relations of a thing.

The creation of parts is a process which is necessarily relativistic: a part depends on its counterpart, or the complement of that part, for its definition (in particular, its extrinsic definition). To state the matter slightly differently, when characterizing a thing with properties or attributes, the *complement* of that thing is also characterized. When everything is divided into something and *not*-something, something has a certain characteristic property in light of which the division is possible in the first place. The *not*-something, on the other hand, does not have that property: further, the not-something *has* the not-property.

For example, consider a table. Now, imagine a part of that table: a table-top thing, which is composed primarily of the surface of the table. In virtue of (conceptually) creating this part, a complementary thing has been created: the legs of the table (i.e. the remainder after the partition). The fact that it is possible to distinguish the table top from the rest of the table implies that it has some property that the rest of the table does not: let us say that it has the property that we can put drinks on it. Because the object has this characteristic property, the complementary object has a complementary property, i.e. the legs of the table have the property that drinks cannot be placed on them. If they did not have this complementary property, then the basis for creating the dichotomy in the first place would disappear (assuming that the table or legs do not have other characteristic properties, which in reality they certainly do).

Under this analysis, the creation of an object is analogous to naming one part of a divided thing: creation is a division in addition to a collection. Every time we create something, we implicitly create at least two somethings. Neither thing is ontologically prior to the other, although we often name only the object on one side of this boundary (which side to name is most often a pragmatic decision). For example, within the context (or superset) of fruits, some subset may be designated as "apple": there is no (simple) designation for the object which is materially constituted by "all fruits that are not apples". So the latter object must be referred to by a complex expression, by negating that which has been named: "non-apple". Note that this negation (or complement-formation) *requires* that we know the whole from which the part was created: a non-apple in the context of "all food" means something other than a non-apple in the context of "all fruits".

It is a mistake to see non-apple things as only lacking in something: possessing the property of being "not-apple" is every bit as characteristic as the concept of apple. Of course, "being a not-apple" may be a less *useful* piece of information compared to "being an apple", because it is a characteristic of a comparatively large number of things. Still, having a property has no more reality than having the opposite of that property, just as the thing apple has no more reality than the thing not-apple (note that we are not talking about the symbols "apple" and "not-apple", where one is a compound word and the other is not). The creation of a decision boundary results in two things, each of which has a characteristic property. Again, which object is named or labeled, as opposed to which object is referred to through negation, is a pragmatic concern. Similarly, the difference in formulation between having a given property and having the negation of that property is a feature of references, not of the things to which those references refer.

Additionally, whether an object possesses a property or not depends on the counterpart of that object. As a concrete example of this conceptual relativism, consider whether "strong people require weak people". In particular, imagine a woman who is strong (e.g. someone in a gym who is lifting a heavy weight). Suppose that her ability remained roughly constant, while everybody else on the planet started weight training, and became capable of lifting weights that she could not lift. If we still called her strong, there would be nobody to call weak anymore. Perhaps we would call everyone else "super-strong", but it seems more likely that we would not call her strong; we would call her weak (even though her ability did not change).

If we do not change the label which we assign to her, the semantics of that label have to be greatly altered. Although we may continue to call her strong, she was relatively strong, and she is now relatively weak. In either case, she is not in control of being weak or strong. Calling her strong depends on other people; it is a relative judgment that depends on the whole of which she is a part. Superman is not super compared to his friends from planet Krypton; he's Regularman.

Some people might maintain that certain attributes of a thing are not relativistic in this sense, or that some attributes have semantics which do not depend on that thing's complement. One example that the scientifically-minded might raise is the mass of an object: the mass of an apple does not depend on the mass of a banana, does it? The banana is not directly used to compute the mass of the apple, but the measure of a thing is always taken with respect to something else. For example, suppose that the mass of the apple is expressed in kilograms. A kilogram is defined as the mass of a certain volume of water at sea level.[8] It is by definition relative; the primary difference between this and the previous example about a given person's strength is that in this case the comparator is a single object (a certain volume of water), whereas in the last example the comparator is a number of objects (other people). Although some choices of measurement may allow consistent application to a wider range of phenomena, there is no *a priori* reason to use one comparator as opposed to another.

Some people may object that the strength of a person may change, but the mass of a specific volume of water does not. To know that the mass of an amount of water does not change, however, we have to weigh it (let us suppose that it weighs one kilogram). In other words, it weighs as much as some other object that weighs one kilogram. If the mass were to change, all we know is that the mass of other objects must have changed at the same time. So we cannot conclude that the mass does not change in an absolute sense, but only that it does not change with respect to something else (unless this is how we define *absolute change* in the first place).

This relativistic viewpoint is closely related to a conundrum proposed by Henri Poincare: if the size of the world doubled overnight, would you notice it? If you assume that all other masses and laws of physics were adjusted as necessary, it is not possible to tell the difference (whether such an undetectable difference is in fact a difference at all is left as an exercise for the reader).

2.4: Dichotomy

Dichotomy both collectivizes and dichotomizes, without being intrusive on the dichotomized domain.

Although the universe may be divided into things, the dividing line itself does not have any concrete existence. Neither do any number of dividing lines: the dividing line itself does not occupy the same *space* that the objects occupy. However, this does not entail that the dividing line is insignificant: it is essential for the formation of sets. Conceptually, there is a difference between a set of apples and a set of pairs of apples, even if these sets ultimately refer to the same apple material (i.e. if they have the same spatial extent). In this section, we explore the nature of the boundary that is created by dichotomy.

Sets and Wholes

Sets are discrete: they may be divided into their members in only one way. Wholes are continuous: they may be divided into further parts in arbitrary ways.

If *something* is created out of everything by a process of dichotomy, then it is a part of everything, but it is not a subset of everything. Hence, there is a very distinct difference between parthood and subsethood. With respect to parts, if my hand is a part of my arm, and my arm is a part of my body, then my hand is a part of my body. With respect to subsets, however, if my hand is a subset of my arm, and my arm is a subset of my body, then it is not true that my hand is a subset of my body: my hand is a subset of a subset of my body. Expressed mathematically, the transitive property does not hold for subsets, but it does hold for (spatiotemporal) things.

Set Theory	Mereology
set	whole
subset	part
union	fusion
intersection	dichotomy (partition)

Table 2.1. Set Theory and Mereology Compared

The table above compares some of the terminology typically associated with set theory and mereology. In general, both sets and wholes are *things*, and both subsets and parts are *somethings*. All of the differences between set theory and mereology are ultimately due to the fact that in set theory, the curly braces have (ontological) significance. In other words, the curly braces cannot be taken away without consequences; they establish a significant boundary, such that the set of a thing is not equivalent to that thing. The set, therefore, is more than the sum of its parts.

Despite the ontological significance of boundaries, however, they are not of the same nature as the things that they collect; they are not parts themselves. To reiterate, sets and subsets have boundaries that are in some sense real, while wholes and parts do not. In both cases, however, the boundaries are not intrusive on the things that they contain (or divide): boundaries, even when they have some reality, are not of the same nature as things. The difference between set boundaries and mereological boundaries is also apparent when we consider collections (either unions or fusions) of subsets and parts: set boundaries are preserved, but mereological boundaries collapse (the parts *fuse* together, which is why a mereological union is known as a fusion). Similarly, intersection (as defined for sets) is not a valid operation on a continuum: hence, a mereological division is referred to as a dichotomy or a partition.

Boundaries

A universe has no boundaries

Universes do not have boundaries; they are by definition unbounded. If a universe did have a boundary, then there would be something in it which it did not contain (and therefore it would not be a universe). In this section, we briefly examine the subjective/objective boundary from the point of view of both the subjective universe and the objective universe.

From the inside of a subjective universe, there are no boundaries: you do not see what you do not see (we cannot experience the objective world in a manner other than that in which it comes to us through our subjective experience). Although you experience a limited subjective world, it is impossible to experience the edge of the subjective world. To be more precise, you can *know* that the subjective world has a boundary or edge, but you cannot perceive it: to perceive an edge as such entails perceiving both of its sides. For example, from the outside, you may view yourself as coextensive with your body. But from the inside, your senses extend right through this boundary; they sense as far as they can, and vision perceives a good deal further than the exterior of the body. So when viewed from the inside, there is no inherent boundary at the edge of your body: in fact, there is no boundary at all.[9]

Similarly, from the outside looking in, there are no boundaries. Psychology has been looking inward (into the brain) for a long time, expecting to find the seat of the soul, but it cannot find the boundary point at which we cross from the objective world into the subjective world.[10] This boundary seems to retreat endlessly, no matter how far into the neural pathways you look. If you look from the outside-in, it looks like sensation continues all the way through (and before you know it, you wind up in action). It may turn out to be somewhat of a doomed endeavor to try to localize a subjective experiencer in the first place, if the boundary between the experiencer and what is experienced does not exist in the way that we think it does.

To summarize a few oddities about this elusive subject: universes themselves have no boundaries, parts of universes are created by boundaries that are not really there, and sets of things are demarcated by boundaries that are there in some sense (although we have not been explicit about their nature).

Truth, Falsity, and Everything in Between

True and false are the essence of categorization.

Many statements may be either true or false: these statements are traditionally called propositions. These statements may not be anything other than true or false: hence, if a statement is not true, then we may infer that the statement is false. If it is not false, then we may infer that the statement is true. In slightly more technical terms, these statements are propositional functions which yield either a true or false result. For example, either an object has the property P_x, or it has the property not-P_x (which we abbreviate by writing $\neg P_x$). The fact that there is no third alternative is known in the field of logic as the Law of the Excluded Middle. This law adds power to our reasoning: it allows us to infer statements on the basis of other statements, which might not otherwise be possible. This law is central to everyday reasoning, and it is closely related to dichotomy.

The law of the excluded middle is not just about binary (true/false) logic. For example, in the field of fuzzy logic, which is an extension of binary logic, the predicates take on true and false values, as well as values in between: for example, statements may be eighty percent true. For example, we may feel that an Asian pear is only somewhat of an apple. If we feel that it is seventy-five percent apple, then the equivalent of the law of the excluded middle in the fuzzy logic context allows us to infer that the Asian pear is twenty-five percent not-apple.[11]

Despite the power of the Law of the Excluded Middle, it is not always applicable. In particular, predicates have a range of valid application, or a set of things to which they can be applied. It is only in the case that a predicate can be validly applied that it divides a set of objects into those objects which have the property and those objects which do not. For example, assume that the predicate "green" can operate effectively only on things which are capable of having a color (i.e. things that emit radiation within the visible spectrum). Particles which are invisible in this sense may not be any color, so it would be meaningless to apply the distinction "green/notgreen" to such particles. If we are determined to apply this predicate, then we are forced to say that:

1. The particle isn't green

2. The particle isn't not-green

However, the combination of both of these statements is problematic under standard logical analysis, where the first statement, "The particle isn't green", may be transformed into "The particle is not-green", which contradicts the second statement.

Therefore, when we invoke the law of the excluded middle, we must be sure to take into account the domain on which the predicate operates. If we wish to be able to conclude that a thing is not-green, we require the following two preconditions:

1. The thing isn't green

2. The predicate green can be applied to the thing (i.e. the thing is in the domain of the function green)

2.5: Dimensions

Dimensions are an extension of the concept of dichotomy.

A dichotomy is the simplest form of dimension, which is just a two-way division. More generally, a dimension can have any number of divisions. In less mathematical contexts, dimensions are also known as *scales*. Scales are typically divided into four types: nominal, ordinal, and interval, and ratio (here, the ratio scale is treated as merely a type of interval scale). These types might also be called unsorted, sorted, and measured dimensions.

Nominal

Nominal dimensions have unordered parts.

A nominal dimension is unordered in the sense that there is no basis to assign relative positions to things. In the figure below, we depict a nominal dimension by showing three things: everything, a named part ("something"), and the complement of that part ("not something"). As this is a nominal dimension, the relative left-right position of the children is not an essential characteristic.[12] For example, if "something" were to the right of "not something" in the diagram below, it would not make a significant difference:

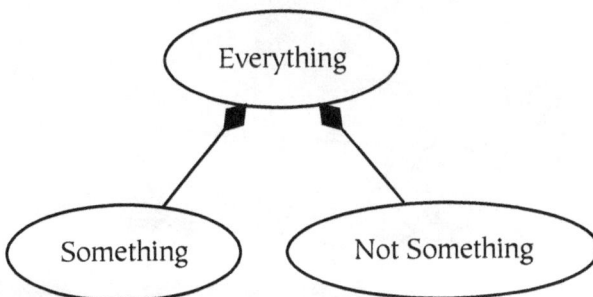

Figure 2.1: Nominal Dimensions

Again, nominal dimensions may determine any number of parts. For a nominal dimension with N parts (or children), we refer to the corresponding division as an N-way division. If the parts do not overlap one another, which is the case for the diagrams in this book, this is also an N-way partition.

Ordinal

Ordinal dimensions are nominal dimensions that have an associated order.

In an ordinal dimension, the relative positions of the divisions have significance. In other words, if a dimension is ordinal, then it imposes an order (or at least a partial order) on the parts that it defines. As an example, finishing first, second, or third in a marathon constitutes an ordinal dimension: knowing the position does not tell you exactly what the winner's time was, it only conveys that one time was greater or less than another.

A diagram depicting an ordinal relationship is shown below, which shows a whole and two parts. We know that child things (parts) must be smaller than their parents, so we are able to determine a *partial order* between the nodes labeled "Whole", "Part" and "Part of a Part" in the figure below. However, although we know that each part is smaller than its parent part, we don't necessarily know any of the sizes:

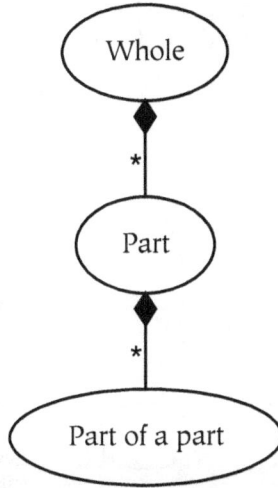

Figure 2.2: Ordinal Dimensions

Part hierarchies, such as the one depicted above, represent ordinal dimensions because the parthood relation (the vertical dimension) imposes a partial order which the horizontal dimension does not. To reiterate, whether one sibling is to the left or right of another is not (structurally) meaningful, whereas it is meaningful to ask if one part is the parent of another.

Interval

Interval dimensions are ordinal dimensions that have an associated measure.

An interval dimension introduces an additional relation between parts that results in a measurable distance (metric) between the designated parts. As a numerical example, 1 is the same distance from 2 as 2 is from 3. One way of creating an interval dimension is to use the same condition for division at each level of the tree. For example, the figure below depicts a structure which is composed of exactly two types of things, a unit element and a sum:

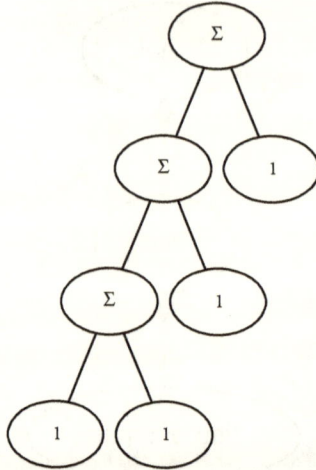

Figure 2.3: Interval Dimensions

Trees which have a fixed metric structure can be described with very few parameters. For example, because every numerical node in the tree above is identical, one can compute the number corresponding to any node in the tree. In the general case, interval dimensions are more flexible than this example illustrates: for example, they need not be linear (e.g. a logarithmic scale could be established by using multiplication instead of addition).

2.6: Hierarchy

A hierarchy is a structure corresponding to successive partitions of a thing.

Hierarchies are collections of dimensions (and simultaneously collections of things). They are tree-like structures, or rather root-like structures, since they branch downwards instead of upwards. Hierarchies often represent divisions of a larger whole, where that whole may be a physical, perceptual, or conceptual thing. Graphically, hierarchies can be produced by grafting trees together in a regular way, or appending the branches of one tree to each of the terminal nodes of the other. For example, consider an object, *x*, which has been divided using two separate dichotomies as follows:

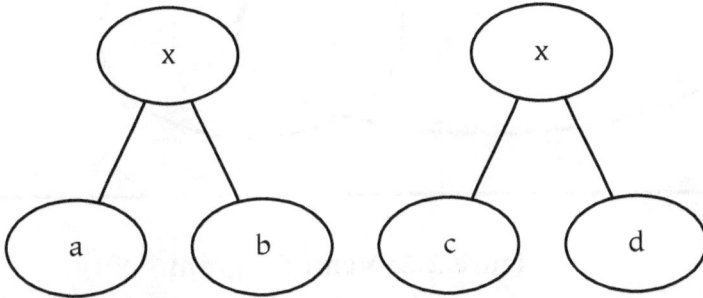

Figure 2.4: Separate Hierarchies

If we wish to combine these two hierarchies, then we may do one of two things. The first possibility is to create a single tree, *x*, with four children corresponding to (ac, ad, bc, bd). However, this does not preserve the notion of priority: if the division into a/b happens before the division into c/d, this information is lost (or at least, it is no longer preserved graphically).[13] If preserving this information about priority is not required, this tree can also be represented with a Venn diagram, which is essentially a flattened tree diagram. A Venn diagram is shown below, where it has been assumed (graphically) that none of the intersections are empty. The labeling of this diagram is not standard, since here the boundaries are labeled (a/b and c/d). The convention for Venn diagrams is to label the parts, which would yield the parts ac, ad, bc, and bd.

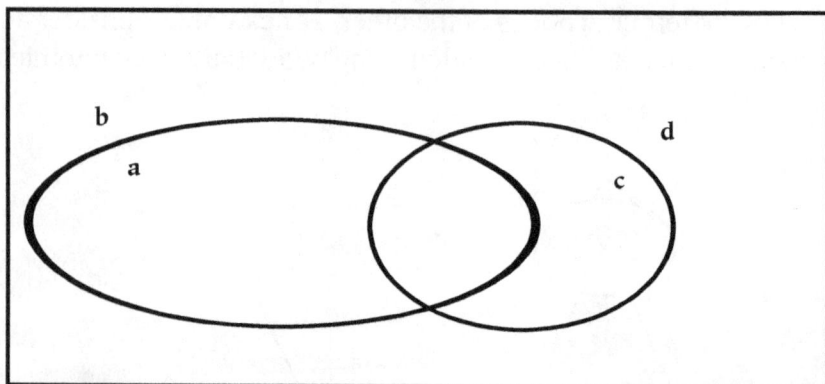

Figure 2.5: Venn Diagram

A second possibility for combining the two dimensions is to append the branches of one tree to each of the terminal nodes of the other tree, which in this case results in three layers of nodes. Each path from the root to a terminal node in this tree can be likened to a mathematical cross-product, where pairs are formed by taking one element from each dimension. This sort of combination increases the depth of the hierarchy, and this additional structure allows one to encode additional information: the divisions closer to the root of the tree are *prior* to those further down.

In some cases, certain of the terminal nodes of the tree will be empty: in those cases, the dimensions were not (entirely) orthogonal. This implies that to some extent, the dimensions encoded the same information. For example, this can happen with the two dichotomies cats/non-cats and animals/non-animals, since there are no cats which are non-animals.[14]

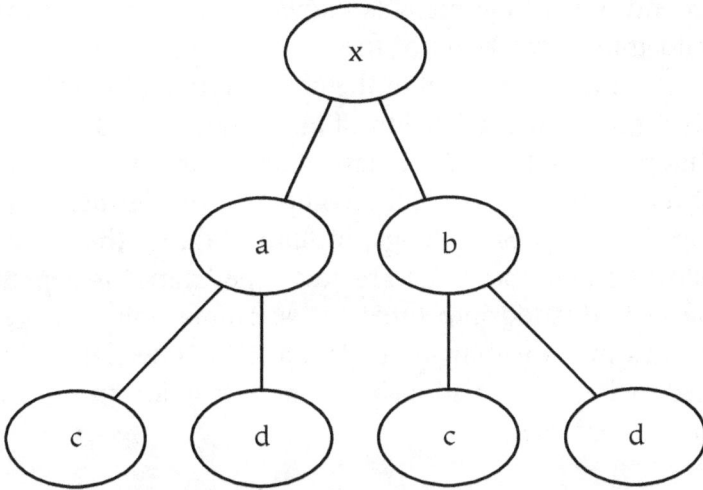

Figure 2.6: Combined Hierarchies

There are two types of common hierarchies which should be carefully distinguished. The first type of hierarchy is known as a *meronomy*, in which the children are *parts* of the parent. In the figure below, a meronomy is depicted in which the whole (the entity at the top of the diagram) is a human body, and the parts are the things that compose or constitute the body. This parthood relationship is denoted with shaded diamond arrowheads:

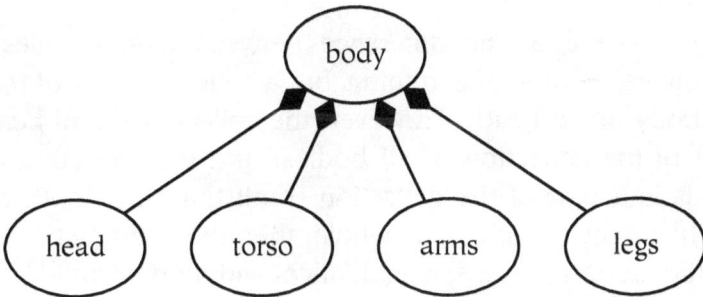

Figure 2.7: A Meronomy

The second type of hierarchy is known as a *taxonomy*, in which the child things are *kinds* of the parent things. A taxonomy is similar to a meronomy in that the collection of all the kinds of a thing is a part of the collection of all things; it is different in the way that parts are formed. Perhaps the most important difference is that a taxonomy is typically composed of *abstract entities*: it is composed of types of things, instead of things themselves. In the following taxonomy, the abstract type "thing" is depicted at the top; it is divided into three types: animal things, vegetable things, and mineral things. To denote this *is-a* relationship, as opposed to the *has-a* relationship of mereonomies, empty triangle arrowheads are used:

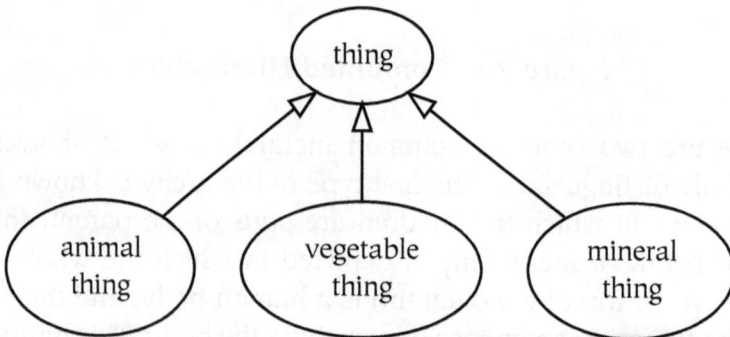

Figure 2.8: A Taxonomy

As an example of the difference between mereonomies and taxonomies, an animal *is-a* thing, but a head *is-a-part-of-a* body (or a body *has-a* head). However, the collection of all heads is a part of the collection of all bodies, and the collection of all animals is a part of the collection of all things. In both cases, if the hierarchy partitions its whole, then the combination of all the children occupies a space identical with that occupied by the parent.

In the following diagram, we represent the extension of the previous (abstract) taxonomy: in other words, the types of the previous taxonomy are represented in this diagram as a set of tokens. An essential difference between this hierarchy and the previous one is that this meronomy consists of nodes which are discontiguous (and plural), while the previous taxonomy consists of nodes which are abstract (and singular). For example, the matter corresponding to "all animals" is distributed in space, as opposed to "animal thing", which is an abstract type as opposed to a physical entity.

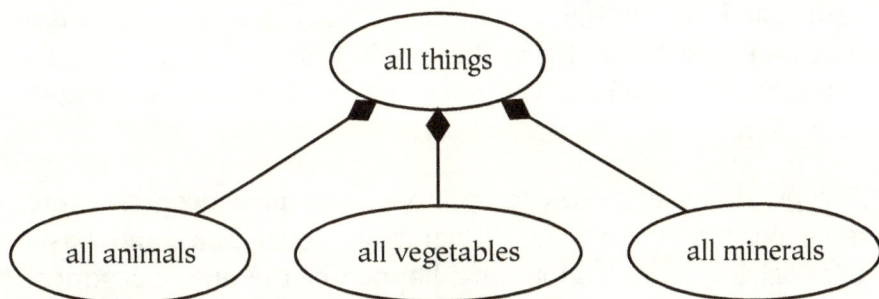

Figure 2.9: A Discontiguous Meronomy

Discontiguous things are often seen to be less *real*, in some sense, then their connected counterparts: hence, nodes in a mereonomy typically represent contiguous quantities. Hence, the previous diagram is often represented with many contiguous nodes, such that all particular animal, vegetable, and mineral things are listed.[15]

Ontological Priority

As concepts occupy positions in ontological hierarchies with a single root, the notion of ontological priority is introduced.

To refer to the fact that one concept is above another in a hierarchy, we say that it is *ontologically prior* to the concept which is lower in the hierarchy (the diagrams in this book follow the convention that knowledge starts at the top). Hence, to understand the origins of knowledge, we should understand which categories are primary, and especially which categories are necessarily primary.

The notion that a hierarchy underlies concepts is an extension of what Noam Chomsky called the *deep structure* of a sentence (the deep structure of a sentence is similar to the tree diagram of a sentence). This deep structure is present in our language, but it is not immediately identifiable (the part of the sentence that is immediately accessible to our perception is known as its *surface structure*). The hierarchy in this book is an extension of deep structure: for example, even nouns have a hierarchy associated with them.

The proximity of nodes to the root node in a deep structure is significant: humans learn hierarchies over time, and basic ontological categorization must happen before finer categorical detail can be achieved. With respect to the syntax of a sentence, the primary division (that occurs at the root of the tree) corresponds to the distinction between the noun phrase and the verb phrase. With respect to our vocabularies, the words that we learn first tend to occur at the top: words which are defined in terms of other words often occur further down in the hierarchy (i.e. as compared to the words which are used to define them). Of particular interest are the types of words or phrases which *necessarily* occur at different ontological levels, as opposed to those that just happen to be learned before others by a given individual. For example, perhaps proper nouns *must* be learned before count nouns, and will therefore necessarily occur at an earlier ontological level.

Although structure and history are to some degree inexorably intertwined, ontological priority is more about structure than it is time of introduction. For example, suppose someone learned the concept "apple" in terms of the concept "fruit". In this scenario, "fruit" is learned before "apple", so for them "fruit" is ontologically prior to "apple". However, if that person has subsequent direct experience with apples, it is no longer the case that "fruit" is necessarily ontologically prior to "apple" (although it remains the first concept to be learned).

Constructing Dimensions

The number of dimensions of a thing is conceptually increased by iterating something along a singleton dimension.

Parts cannot have a dimensionality which is different than the space that contains them. Therefore, increasing the dimensionality of an existing universe by collecting a large number of objects (or reducing the dimensionality by slicing a thing along one of its existing dimensions) is not strictly possible.

However, references to things, understood from within the referential domain (i.e. understood *as references* instead of *as parts*), may have a dimensionality which is different than the dimensionality of the things to which they refer. Further, the references themselves may be collected in a referential space. The effect of doing so is to increase the dimensionality of the things, by abstracting over them.

We will return to the topic of references in future sections, since they have not yet been formally introduced. For now, the increase in dimensionality will be depicted with atoms. Atoms should be conceived of as having a atomic extent in a large number of dimensions (as opposed to a zero size, which is the case for mathematical points). This extent is similar to how one might conceive of a piece of paper: although we may treat it as a two-dimensional object in a large number of contexts, it is actually of a higher dimensionality (otherwise adding pages to a book would not add thickness).

In the figures below, we show the process of adding dimensions to an atomic entity (i.e. one which has no parts). In the first figure, there is simply an atom: it has no extent which can be further subdivided along any dimension. To turn this description around: since it is not possible to sub-divide an atom, an atom does not have any dimensionality.

•

Figure 2.10: An Atom: Zero Dimensions

In Figure 2.11, "A Line: One Dimension", we iterate the object shown in the first figure, in a direction which is orthogonal to any non-atomic extents already present (which is easy to do for an atom, since it cannot have orientation). In this way, we end up with a line:

Figure 2.11: A Line: One Dimension

This process is repeated to create the second and third dimensions, corresponding to Figure 2.12, "A Plane: Two Dimensions" and Figure 2.13, "A Space: Three Dimensions". In the first case, many lines, iterated over a new dimension, can be represented as a plane. In the second case, many planes, indexed by a new (orthogonal) dimension, form a three-dimensional space (which may be envisioned as a cube).

Figure 2.12: A Plane: Two Dimensions

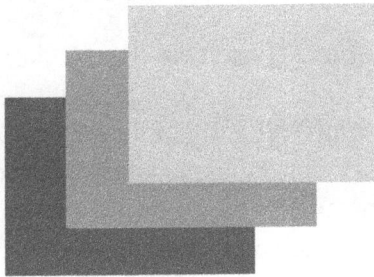

Figure 2.13: A Space: Three Dimensions

The fourth dimension is time. In other words, time may be conceived of as simply another (spatial) dimension. Of course, we seem to move in it in only one direction, so our behavior with respect to it is different. We certainly perceive it differently (if in fact it is perceived, as opposed to being conceived), and we treat it very differently linguistically, but there is no reason to believe that it is of an altogether different nature than the first three spatial dimensions. In fact, it is treated almost identically in modern physical equations dealing with spacetime. In any case, as with the previous dimensions, this novel dimension is introduced by iterating a lower-dimensional object along a new axis, which is orthogonal to those which exist so far.

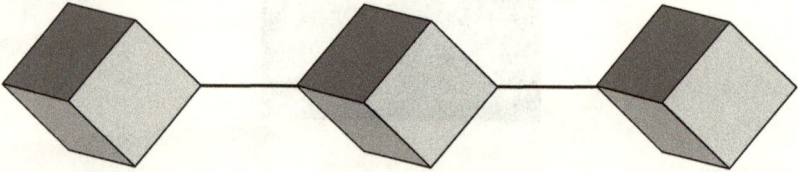

Figure 2.14: A Timeline: Four Dimensions

There are some objects, such as the Necker Cube, which have four *spatial* dimensions, none of which is a temporal dimension. Such objects are quite difficult to visualize, precisely because of interposing another spatial dimension between the typical three spatial dimensions and the temporal dimension. Perhaps the use of a fourth spatial dimension (instead of the temporal dimension) is desirable because the temporal dimension is perceived in a radically different way than the spatial dimensions. One motivation for not acknowledging time as the fourth (spatial) dimension could be due to the constraints or tendencies of language (and thought). In particular, perhaps there are syntactic constraints that encourage us to extend the dimensionality of noun phrases, rather than add dimensionality to the verb phrase (the analogy between nouns/verbs and space/time is explored in greater detail later in the book).

In any case, despite the fact that the behavior of matter in time is very different that its behavior in space, we will persist in calling time simply the fourth dimension, which downplays its status as a different type of dimension. The ordering of dimensions themselves is a matter of convenience: mapping time to the fourth dimension is an attempt to preserve the order of dimensions that appears most natural (of course, this notion of *naturalness* may be a bias inherited from the English language, in which the subject comes before the verb).

The depiction of a five-dimensional object is a particularly interesting example of how each successive dimension is produced, because few of us have (at least explicitly) extended our conceptualization of dimensionality that far. Although all of us can picture three dimensions easily, and the intrepid among us can picture four without too much difficulty, the idea of the fifth dimension seems somewhat incomprehensible at best (and at worst, the subject of a bad science fiction novel).

Implicitly, however, we use the fifth dimension all the time. To conceptualize the five-dimensional world, picture this: there is another earth, similar but not exactly the same as ours. It exists at the same place (spatial coordinates) as our earth, and it exists at the same time (temporal coordinate) as our earth. However, we do not trip over the things of that earth: that earth exists in another dimension (i.e. it occupies a different fifth dimensional ordinate).[16] Implicitly, this dimension is used in our language to represent possibility: possible worlds or possible life histories. For example, if we speak of free will, conscious volition is that which is used to *choose* one or another ordinate on this dimension. As the dimension of possibility, we make use of the fifth dimension all the time; it is not a difficult concept to grasp (even though it is not explicitly spoken of as a spatial dimension). So, if the four dimensions are sufficient to describe a world-line, the fifth dimension allows the representation of multiple world-lines. The introduction of the fifth dimension enables the possibility of discussing *possible* worlds, so we will refer to the fifth dimension as the dimension of modality.[17]

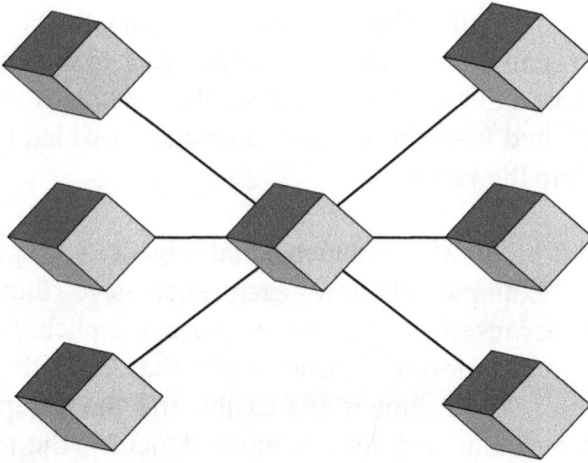

Figure 2.15: Multiple Timelines: Five Dimensions

Notes

[1] It is a rather modern family, in which no child has more than one parent.

[2] Dimensions tend to characterize certain perspectives. Objects may be obtained by partitioning and recombining a whole in numerous different ways, so the selection of a particular partitioning strategy is generally motivated by a particular desire or perspective. Analogously, the parts into which a thing is decomposed are those parts that are relevant to the analysis which is being carried out. If you are hungry, you will look for food objects; if your only tool is a hammer, you will partition reality in virtue of its resemblance to nails.

[3] Whether one labels parts or not is a pragmatic decision. For a *proper* partition of an entity, at least two parts are created (both the part and the complement of that part are nonempty), and either or both parts may be named. If only one part is named, then the complement is denoted as the negation of the named part.

[4] In other words, even if the separation of a thing into parts creates only connected entities, the collection of certain of these separated parts into a larger thing may create a thing which is not (topologically) connected.

[5] Mathematically inclined readers who are interested in approaches to mathematics which do not rely on the notions of infinity and point-sets may be interested in intuitionist mathematics and point-free topologies. Several introductory references may be found at http://www.cognitivesettheory.com/links

[6] We should note that this is a relatively simplistic characterization: there is a large body of literature examining the difference between intrinsic/extrinsic properties.

[7] Since everything is all-inclusive, it can have no extrinsic properties: there is nothing outside of it with which to relate it. Neither does it have intrinsic properties, as it is considered as a whole (i.e. unless we are subdividing it, we cannot give an intrinsic description). So, we say that it is beyond description (and apologize for describing it by saying that it is beyond description).

[8] At least this was the original definition of the kilogram: the mass of a liter of water at sea level. Since that mass can vary, the kilogram was subsequently defined in terms of International Prototype Kilogram, a particular object located in France. Since the mass of *that* object has also been found to vary, the kilogram is currently being redefined.

[9] Note that we are considering boundaries to be things which divide one thing from another: the notion of an edge with only one side is paradoxical.

[10] Many psychologists expected to find something they called a homunculus, which literally means "little person": it represents some smaller agent at the controls of the body, perhaps located in the brain. This type of thinking is paradoxical if it leads to the expectation that homunculi must themselves have homunculi.

[11] Another context in which negation finds a home is in set theory, where negation is represented as the set complement operation. Complementation plays the same

role (in terms of forming a Boolean logic) as negation, although it generalizes to more entities than just true or false.

[12]The fact that the order of the children is not meaningful is also a characteristic of mathematical sets.

[13]If we regard the names of the nodes as significant, then this information is still preserved (although it may no longer be inferred from the structure of the tree).

[14]On the other hand, if the nodes at the same level overlap, then they were not the result of a partition. Unless otherwise mentioned, the part hierarchies in this book are partitions.

[15]Diagrammatically, this is indicated with a Kleene star (or an asterisk) next to the node. The Kleene star indicates that there may be a number of instances of the thing that is associated with the star.

[16]Keep in mind that we are talking about conceptual dimensions here: this is how our cognitive landscape is structured. The fifth dimension is a dimension of our thought, regardless of whether it is also a dimension of the physical universe.

[17]Be aware that calling the fifth dimension the dimension of modality, or even talking about the fifth dimension to someone other than a physics geek, is not a common practice.

Chapter 3: Nothing

"Nothing" is a reference which does not refer to something.

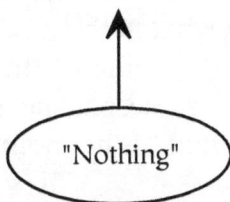

In this diagram, "nothing" is depicted as a reference, by showing an arrow pointing towards the referent of "nothing": nothing. "Nothing" is unique as references go, since it is not a reference to something.

3.1: Nothing

"Nothing" is the complement of "everything"

One of the most interesting things, about which whole books have been written, is nothing. It can be quite a challenge to talk about nothing, despite the success of a select few. On one hand, it is impossible for us to say what nothing is, since nothing does not exist. On the other hand, "nothing" (the word that represents nothing) certainly does exist, despite the fact that its referent does not. In other words, "nothing" is not nothing.[1]

"Nothing" means *no thing* in the domain of discourse. It becomes rather elusive when it is taken to exist, in the sense that "nothing" is something. According to our definition, it is not the case that nothing is something; nothing is not something. So is nothing nothing? If it is not yet clear, it is easy to get caught in a substantial semantic quagmire by talking about nothing.[2]

"Nothing" is a reference which does not validly reference something. Everything was previously defined by saying that it occupies every position along every dimension which was used to characterize that domain. Nothing, the complement of everything, necessarily occupies *no* position along *any* dimension. Hence, it does not exist: the reference to it, however, does exist (otherwise we could not talk about it, or even ask if it existed). As nothing does not exist, it cannot be said to have any properties (or lack any properties). It is tempting to say that it has the property of not existing, but existence is a property only of references, not of the things to which they refer.[3]

At first glance, the utility of a concept which does not correspond to anything in the real world does not seem terribly high. Why would I say that "I have zero of something" as opposed to saying "I do not have something"? The former formulation contradicts the notion of "having". Despite these objections, it is sometimes convenient for a language to have a *zero-element*. If a language has references, but it does not have the reference known as nothing, then it is more difficult to talk about mental things which do not exist. Things which do not exist are all denotationally equivalent, both to each other and to the reference nothing. For example, if one is asked how many people have set foot on Mars, and an answer is mandatory, then the concept of zero is required (which is a near analogue of nothing).

3.2: References

References form the basis for points of view.

The introduction of "nothing" into our domain of discourse forces us to take account of references (as "nothing" is such a thing). References are both things in themselves, as well as things which refer to other things. The significance of references most often derives not from what they are, but from what they represent. For example, the firing of a neuron might be an electrical discharge, but it might *mean* that a cat is rubbing up against our leg. From a subjective viewpoint, the neuronal activity is not merely associated with something else: it *is* something else.

References depend on interpretation, or the adoption of a certain point of view: although they can be understood in terms of what they are materially, they are references because they can substitute for the thing to which they refer. The semantics of a situation are altered by taking things at face value, as opposed to understanding those things as references to other things. In virtue of this, references form the basis of different points of view of the same phenomena.

In the field of semiotics, two primary kinds of references are distinguished: signs and symbols. Signs are things which *point to* something else. For example, an arrow painted on the ground points to (signifies) something else; it does not point to itself.

Symbols, on the other hand, stand for (or represent) something else. For example, words are in some sense substitutable for the things they reference. In this book, the term "references" encompasses both signs and symbols.

The term "reference" is convenient because of the symmetric notion of dereferencing. If a reference to a thing is dereferenced, the original thing is once again obtained. For example, if x is the name for y, then we may say that x references y, or that x is a reference to y. We might also say that x denotes y, or that y is denoted by x.

Notational and Denotational Equivalence

References may differ, even though the things they refer to are the same.

In some situations, the hierarchy which is responsible for carving a particular part out of a larger whole is arbitrary. For example, one may wish to identify green tomatoes. Two parthood derivations that identify a thing that is green, which is also a tomato, are depicted in the following two figures. The diagram labeled "Green Tomatoes" illustrates a hierarchy where green/notgreen is ontologically prior to tomato/nottomato, and the diagram labeled "Tomatoes, Green" shows the alternative scenario (where tomato/nottomato is ontologically prior to green/ notgreen):

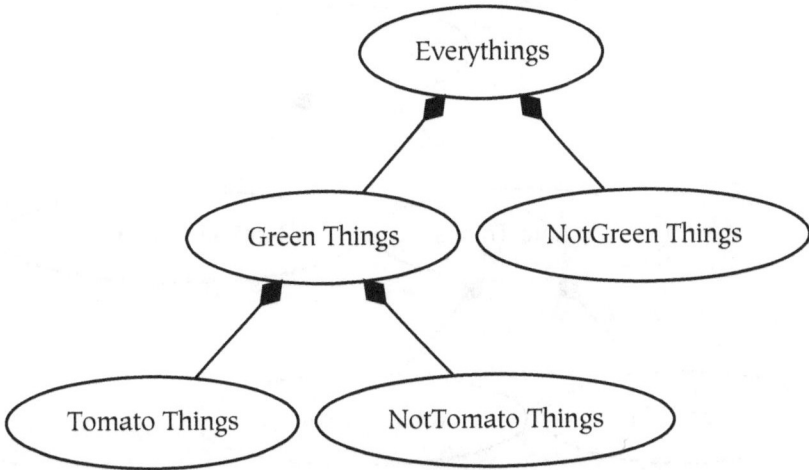

Figure 3.1: Green Tomatoes

The things identified by the bottom left node in figures 3.1 and 3.2 are the same: *greenish tomatoey things,* or alternatively, *tomatoey greenish things* (neglecting the fact that "tomatoey" has somewhat looser membership criteria than "tomatoes"). In both cases, the referenced concept must be constructed from other words, so it takes at least two hierarchical levels to create (i.e. we do not have a single concept for green tomatoes). From the awkwardness of the latter construction, it seems that most English speakers would derive this thing as in figure 3.2, where the category tomato is prior to color.[4]

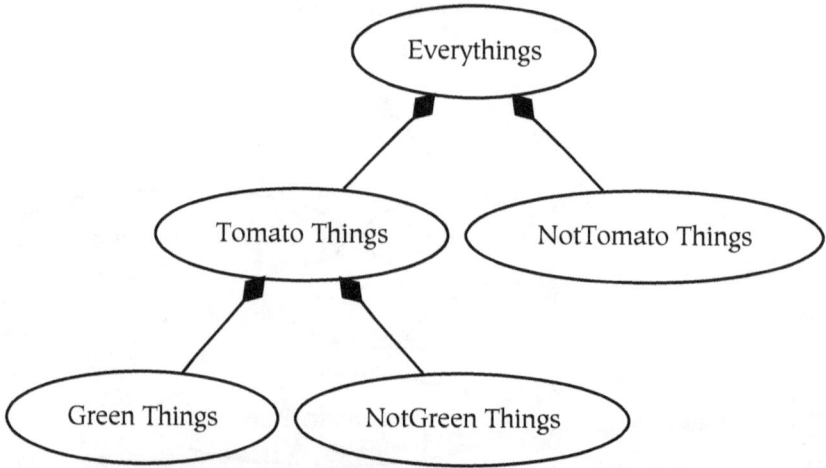

Figure 3.2: Tomatoes, Green

The substitutability of the nodes that represent nouns and adjectives is coincident with treating them as similar things on a conceptual level. In particular, nouns and adjectives are both understood as conceptual functions that apply to space. The significant difference is that nouns have already been applied to that spatial thing, while adjectives still require that spatial thing (which is exactly why they require nouns).

Although most people would not be surprised to find such a conceptual simplification, some people might advocate for treating adjectives like nouns ("green things") instead of like functions ("green"). This approach, which is the one taken by first order logic, poses a number of problems for natural language. For example, if we treat "small" as equivalent to the set of small objects, then we must be able to enumerate the set of small objects. However, if we include objects such as small apples in the set of small things, it poses a problem because these objects are huge when compared to large cherries. In other words, treating adjectives as nouns does not account for *context sensitivity*: sets of small things can be enumerated only after knowing the domain to which they apply.

Encoding Information

References encode small amounts of information about the referenced domain.

Evolution rewards animals which can represent and make use of an immense amount of information, as long as the biological cost of this representation is not too great. Hence, the compression of information is of great value. That compression entails the use of references to encode information. References are easy to manipulate as opposed to the things that they reference, so their use is certainly convenient. If we wish to represent the world in a smaller part of itself, the use of concise references is mandatory: otherwise the contained thing would have to be as large as its container. In other words, references (or words) are a means of signal compression. This view of language offers a number of insights into the nature of human language and thought, two of which are briefly explored here.

One insight is that the use of symbols to encode information makes the distribution of the symbols critically important. For example, if there is no snow in the world, then there is little use for words that describe snow. If there are numerous kinds of snow, sleet, and hail, then this variety would entail a large number of symbols to represent it accurately: in practice, this is exactly what happens.[5]

The other significant insight derives from the fact that signal compression is often achieved by means of dimensionality reduction. The key observation behind reducing the number of dimensions in order to compress information is that much of the change in an event happens only in a few of the dimensions which that event occupies. For example, if some object moves from here to there, there are many dimensions of the object which do not change (such as the dimensions which take account of only its internal structure). Because the dimensions of variation are primarily those related to the position of that object, we can represent the change using only those dimensions: the other dimensions are not significant.

By not describing the variation along dimensions which change by relatively insignificant amounts, it is possible to both achieve a great simplicity in representation and also discard very little significant information. Of course, the determination of *which* information is significant can be difficult: from some points of view the object is changing so much that it does not even make sense to consider it the same object: from other points of view, these same changes can effectively be ignored. In practical terms, although there is some risk in discarding important information, a large amount of compression can be achieved if the dimensions of change are chosen carefully.[6]

3.3: Existence

Existence refers to the possibility of validly dereferencing concepts.

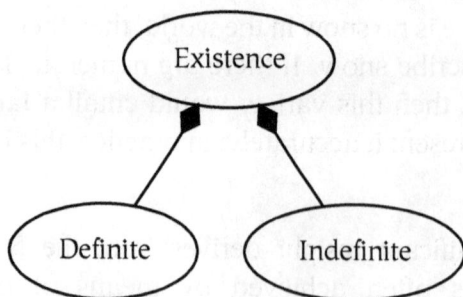

For a reference to exist means that the referent occupies some non-zero amount of space. If this is the case, we will also say that the concept can be *validly dereferenced*: it refers to something, as opposed to nothing.

Existence is a property only of references: existence means that a reference can be validly dereferenced. As non-referential things cannot be dereferenced, it is meaningless to ask if non-referential things exist. As an example, consider the following question: "Does the apple exist?". This is a reasonable question if the term "apple" is being used as a reference (or a linguistic variable); in that case, the answer is true if it is possible to find the apple in the world. This is not a reasonable question if it is asking whether an apple-in-the-world exists, since under that reading of the sentence, the phrase apple-in-the-world presupposes existence.[7] In either case, it is interesting to note the facility with which we dereference references, especially since this process happens somewhat unconsciously.

There are at least two kinds of existence and nonexistence: necessary and contingent. For example, as necessity and contingency apply to nonexistence, there are things that do not exist because they are not valid conceptual forms (such as colorless green things) and things that do not exist because they happen not to exist (such as the people on mars). The former concepts do not exist as a matter of necessity: they cannot exist in virtue of their conceptual (or linguistic) construction. A popular example of things that cannot exist are self-referential concepts, which have an impossible deep structure. The latter kind of concepts, or contingently non-existent concepts, simply happen not to exist: there is no reason in principle why they could not.

Both necessary and contingent existence, however, assume a potentially perfect correspondence between references and the things to which they refer. The reality of the situation is often less black and white. A more subtle kind of existence (or lack thereof) occurs when the reference does not correspond exactly to its referent. For example, objects might exist in a different way than their associated concepts exist. Similarly, the question of existence is often not a determination of *if* concepts and objects correspond, but *how* concepts and objects correspond. For example, how does our *percept* 'apple' correspond to the *object* apple?

One way in which objects and concepts differ is that objects do not exist as physically singular entities in the way that our conceptions of them do. So to the extent that a particular conceptual partition into atomic entities prevents other partitions or points of view, that point of view cannot reflect the totality of reality. For example, if we see people as individuals, it may block our view of them as collections of cells, or as parts of a larger social organism. The world, since it is capable of being conceptually partitioned in any number of ways, cannot be entirely understood on the basis of only one of these partitions.

3.4: Identity

For two things to be called the same thing implies the notion of identity.

There are at least two criteria for identity. One criteria is bottom-up, according to which two things are the same thing if they are composed of the same parts. The other criteria is top-down, according to which two things are the same thing if they are parts of the same larger wholes. When references are considered, additional criteria must be introduced to establish identity conditions between different referential expressions, as well as the conditions between references and the things that they reference. The rest of this chapter looks at the concept of identity from these different perspectives.

Two things are identical when they satisfy all of the conditions for identity: both internal and external. However, these identity conditions entail that nothing is identical with anything else (things are only identical with themselves, and the world is full of either one or many unique individuals, depending on how one conceives of it). Therefore, it is necessary to loosen the conditions for identity in practice. In fact, knowing how these conditions should be loosened and how they should remain strict is exactly what constitutes learning the nature of things.

Spatial Identity

Knowing a thing's identity requires knowing the spatial boundaries of that thing.

Identity is defined spatially: to know a thing's identity requires knowing its boundaries (at a minimum). The spatial conditions are slightly different from the material conditions for identity, which says that things are the same if they are made of the same material. Another way of expressing material identity is to say that things are the same if they are made up of the same parts. A spatial notion of identity adds to this that things are the same if they are parts of the same larger wholes: it adds an extrinsic condition for identity.

In order to distinguish material and spatial identity, it is important to understand "being composed of the same parts" in a particular way. For example, although a car may be composed of a body and four wheels, it should not be understood only as the set of these parts: if that were the case, these parts may be randomly arranged and still constitute the same thing. The wheels, if they are stacked on top of the car, do not constitute the same object as the car in a more drivable configuration. In terms of parts, although both cars consist of wheels and a body, only one of these two configurations has a part which is axle-and-wheels (as a contiguous object). These cars are not the same in terms of their functional (extrinsic) relationships, either, since one of the cars will not roll down the road.

Most objects, or at least most objects that humans identify, possess clear spatial boundaries: a division can be made between an object and its environment which serves to delimit the object from what it is not. Although for many objects the boundary appears quite clear cut, boundaries are potentially quite complex. For example, knowing what an apple is requires knowing the boundary between apple and non-apple. At a macroscopic level, this is not too difficult: whether the stem or the leaf are parts of the apple is fairly easy to decide, at least in principle. At a microscopic level, it becomes less and less clear which parts belong to which object (for example, it is probably unclear to which object a given electron belongs).[8]

The objects that concepts refer to often *stick together* in space and through time: they are spatiotemporally contiguous. In some cases, this continuity of form may be very definite, like the shape of a diamond. In other cases, the shape may be more of a fluid connectedness, such as a puddle of water which is viewed as one thing, despite the fact that its shape may change greatly over its lifetime.[9] Some objects may even be discontinuous (although in this case, their status as singular objects is somewhat contentious). One example is that of an ant colony: from a linguistic point of view, an ant colony is singular. In terms of the objects which constitute that thing, the colony is composed of a plurality of ants.[10] However, the ant colony is also a single, concrete object, which just happens to be spatially discontiguous.

Temporal Identity

Knowing a thing's identity requires knowing the temporal boundaries of that thing.

On the one hand, time should be regarded as simply a fourth spatial dimension. On the other hand, since time is so cognitively different than the other (spatial) dimensions, it is worth treating separately.

Now we are reading a page. *Now*, a second later, are we reading the *same* page? Although it is slightly different than it was just a moment ago (it has different atoms, a different molecular arrangement, and has been read once more, etc), we would still conventionally say that we are looking at the same page. The debate over what exactly constitutes identity through time is an old one: maintaining strict requirements for temporal identity led Xenophanes, a citizen of ancient Greece, to state:

You cannot step into the same river twice.

One of the more famous puzzles pertaining to the notion of identity also comes from Greece, and is called "the ship of Theseus".[11] The puzzle begins with the following conditions:

1. At one point and time, Theseus had a ship.

At this point, we know what Theseus's ship is (or at least we think we do).

2. The gods didn't like Theseus much, and as a result, his ship had to be repaired quite frequently.

At this point, even though some pieces of the boat have been replaced, most people have no hesitation saying (and believing) that it is the same ship.

3. Eventually, every piece of the original ship had been replaced.

At this point, the question of whether this is the same ship is a bit more difficult to answer. Most people probably maintain that it is still the same ship. However, it contains none of the original matter; all of the wood is different wood. If we maintain that the ship is the same, then we must be using criteria other than material criteria; we must believe that being composed of the same stuff is not a necessary condition for identity.

4. Theseus' evil twin, Feceus, collects all of the original pieces and builds a ship from these pieces.

At this point, there are two ships: but which of the two ships is the *real* ship of Theseus? Is one, or the other, or neither, or both, the ship(s) of Theseus? This uncomfortable choice might lead us to tease apart the concept of the ship of Theseus into two concepts: the same-material ship and the enduring-shape ship. If we do *not* tear our original concept apart (just as the gods tore apart the ship itself), we must settle for a rather one-sided view of things. Further, in case we think that the question about the identity conditions for a boat are irrelevant, we might consider other objects whose material is similarly swapped out (such as the cells of our body, which are supposedly replaced every seven years).

Given the large number and kinds of conditions for identity, it seems misconceived to form a rigid concept of the enduring, single, ship-of-Theseus. This example illustrates at least two good (and separable) criteria: being composed of the same material and the persistence of shape. Functional similarity is another popular criterion: the ship of Theseus may be defined as any ship that Theseus happens to own or sail on at a given time. There are many others, which points to the fact that any single criterion seems to be lacking.

Concepts which reference (or apply to) their object in an all-or-none fashion, such as being a particular boat, are made even more black and white by simple, rational identity criteria. This binary logic which dictates whether or not a concept applies to an object often does not correspond very well to the underlying reality of the situation. The change in underlying processes is relatively continuous, so our attempts to deal with these processes conceptually often results in rigid (or discrete) approximations.

Again using an apple as an example, we might ask: when did the apple begin? It was probably "not an apple" when it was unmixed flower and pollen. Even after these two mixed, most people would still not call it an apple. Does it instantaneously become an apple when there are 2, 4, or 8 cells? It seems problematic to hold that there is no apple, and then, at some instant in time, there is an apple. One alternative to defining this precise instant of creation might be to apply *fuzzy* temporal borders to concepts. In other words, the pollinated flower is not *very much* an apple, but it is *somewhat* an apple. As the apple develops, it becomes more of an apple; when it is ripe and ready to eat, is so much of an apple that we simply say it *is* an apple: one-hundred percent. In this case the apple, just before it was an apple, was not a non-apple; it was somewhat of an apple. Of course, fuzzy object boundaries do not make all of the issues involved with identity disappear; they just make those issues fuzzy, too.

The uncertainty at the beginning of the apple's existence is similar to the uncertainty at its end. If the apple falls off the tree and slowly composts, it does not cease existing as an apple at a given instant. This process may happen rapidly, but it does not happen instantaneously. It tends to become less and less of an apple until it is indistinguishable from the ground; or at least until it becomes something else. Perhaps it is not a coincidence that things tend to go out of existence when there is another category or word to which they belong a little better. For example, if we had a single word for "rotten apple" (e.g. rapple), it seems likely that apples would be doomed to live less long than they do now: they would cease to exist as soon as they became rapples (although of course, some people would argue that we would create the term "rapple" precisely because we recognized such an object in the world).[12]

To summarize, the beginning and the end of an object in the world often seem relatively continuous (at least up to the quantum level). Our percepts of the object are crude approximations of this underlying continuity (as neurons are much larger than subatomic particles). By contrast, the beginning and end of a concept are even more discrete. Although the sharp transition at the entry to or exit from a concept can be softened with various linguistic hedges, concepts most often either *apply to an object* or *do not apply*. Under this condition, it seems that categorization leads to categorical understanding, even if the objects so categorized are not inherently categorical things.

Referential Identity

Two references are *referentially identical* if they have the same referent.

A single thing may be described on many levels, all of which are equally valid. For example, here are several descriptions of an apple, given by people in different lines of work:

· Sociologist: "The apple is a kind of food-stuff to be fed to the masses by the proletariat to keep them from revolting."

· Psychologist: "The apple often stops the hunger neurons from firing, thus contributing to the cessation of the apple-gathering response."

· Biologist: "The apple is a fruit, whose sweetness has been selected by evolution to provide for the disbursement and fertilization of the tree's dicotyledonous progeny."

· Chemist: "The apple is a complex of medium-chain, starchy hydrocarbons. It contains approximately twenty grams of fructose."

· Physicist: "The apple contains primarily carbon, hydrogen, and oxygen. It warps spacetime in virtue of its mass."

These statements are contrived to indicate that the nature of the apple depends on the observer's perspective. They indicate that the apple is defined by the relations into which it enters, and illustrate several of an unlimited number of these relations as emphasized by people in different professions. These different levels of description do not require different observers; they could be descriptions made by a single observer at different times. The observer-when-hungry will categorize the apple as something to eat (a sweet fruit); the same observer might later categorize the apple as something on which to do experiments (an uncomplaining test subject). These different levels of description are not necessarily exclusive of each other: they are just different points of view, each of which uses its own terminology. In practice, however, it is difficult to conceive of different points of view at the same time.

Isomorphic Identity

A reference has a valid correspondence to a referenced thing if their respective relations in each universe are identical.

Identity conditions have been given for both things which are not references and things which are references. But what are the conditions under which references correctly apply to the things to which they intend to refer?

Clearly, strict identity conditions are not adequate: as examined in the last section, even two references to the same thing are not identical. References and the things to which they refer are different in kind: the concept of apple is not at all like the object apple. Even references to references are somewhat different than references to objects. On the other hand, the concept of apple does not apply to the object of orange, so there are also clearly valid and invalid mappings between these two things.[13]

Subjective references are identical to their referents in virtue of the mathematical concept of isomorphism. Isomorphism comes from the words for "same" (iso) and "shape" (morph). If concepts are represented with tree structures, this term can be understood as a graph isomorphism: a reference correctly maps to a thing if and only if that reference occurs in the same position in a tree of references that the thing occupies in a tree of referred-to things. For example, consider the relative conceptual position of "apple" in the diagram below:

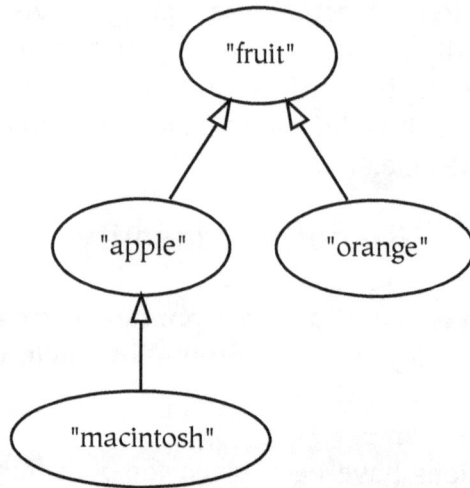

If the world of fruit corresponds to this picture (which might be verified through observation and talking to other people), then the concept "apple" and the object apple are isomorphic: we can validly impose a structure on the world that resembles this structure, even if the nodes in each domain are composed of entirely different stuff. In other words, because isomorphism is the only requirement, it is not necessary to have any relation other than congruence between objects and concepts: the concept of green does not require any intrinsic resemblance to a green object.

Just as with spoken language, in which arbitrary words can be associated with arbitrary concepts, random collections of neurons can map to arbitrary things in the world. The reference itself does not need to intrinsically correspond to the form of the thing to which it refers: only the relationships into which it enters must be the same. In fact, even the nature of the referential space may be different than the nature of the referenced space. For example, the referential space may be discrete, even though the space which is referred to is continuous.

Notes

[1]"Nothing" is a valid concept, but it does not correspond to anything in the world (it has no spatial extent). So, it is a reference, but it is not a valid reference.

[2]The lack of a clear denotation for the referential level of a thing is probably responsible for much of the confusion about nothing. There is a distinct difference between a thing and a reference to that thing. This book uses quotes to denote the latter, such that "apple" is a reference to 'apple'.

[3]If existence were not restricted to references, it would presuppose existence just to talk about something.

[4]This comparison ignores the fact that green and tomato are different parts of speech. However, ontological priority is inextricably connected with creating parts of speech in the first place. For English, one means of codifying ontological priority in language is by making the ontologically-prior thing a noun, and the ontologically-subsequent thing an adjective. Syntactically, this corresponds to the fact that nouns can operate as noun phrases, but adjectives cannot.

[5]The linguist Benjamin Whorf gathered information about this phenomenon: he found that Alaskan natives had seventeen different words for snow, while speakers of most other languages have many fewer. This particular evidence is relatively famous because it is tied to what is called the Sapir-Whorf hypothesis. In a weak formulation, this hypothesis states that language enables thought, so that possessing a rich language about a given subject allows more detailed or precise thought about that subject.

[6]It makes sense to reduce dimensionality for the purposes of conveying an event. However, the listener must not make the assumption that the event itself is a low-dimensional thing; only the characterization of it is of low dimensionality (which is required for symbolic communication).

[7]To even speak of things like apple-in-the-world is problematic, because in virtue of their being spoken about they become referential expressions: that is the nature of language. The ontological argument for the existence of God is a wonderful example of this issue. However, there may be an unspoken immediacy of experience about which one cannot ask, and of which it is incorrect to conceive of as either existing or not existing (as it is not referential): of course, we could not talk about it if there were.

[8]To further cloud the issue, recent physics experiments have shown that some properties of one object are *instantaneously* affected by altering an object at some distance from the first object at the level of very small particles. Although there are several ways in which to explain this finding, some physicists simply deny the independence of these entwined objects. In other words, they maintain that there is one object, which has spatially distributed components.

[9]Spatial boundaries, although they are fairly easy to identify, may not be the essential boundaries of a thing. W.V.O. [Quine] uses the example of a cat named

Tibbles, whose boundary initially seems quite well-defined. However, if through some incident Tibbles' tail is cut off, then it is not clear if both parts are Tibbles, or if Tibbles refers only to the cat part and not the tail part (in the latter case, the tail was a nonessential part of Tibbles).

[10]Another (perhaps more convincing) example is a supercomputing cluster with wireless Ethernet connections. The cluster is in some sense a singular machine, potentially computing a single function, using hardware which is connected only by the transmission of information.

[11]Theseus was a sailor from Greece whose ship was repeatedly smashed by the gods.

[12]This example is similar to Zeno's paradox of the heap: if one has a heap of sand, and grains are removed one at a time, at what point is the heap no longer a heap? It seems counterintuitive to say that a single grain of sand can make the difference between a heap and a non-heap. If we conclude that a single grain of sand does not make the difference, we probably think of "heaps" as concepts which can apply to the things they describe to a greater or lesser degree, as opposed to being strictly binary predicates.

[13]References and the things to which they refer occupy different (referential) universes. The relation between references and the things that they reference is one of the bigger topics in philosophy: it is often encountered during discussions of dualism and qualia. Dualism (and monism) is a discussion about how the physical world relates to the mental world, and qualia is a discussion about the subjective experience of phenomena.

Part II: Universes

There are three well-known universes: the objective universe, the perceptual universe, and the conceptual universe.

There are three different universes: the physical universe, the subjective universe, and the conceptual universe. In addition to viewing each universe as an independent and complete whole, these universes (or references to parts of them) may be viewed as parts of one another (in this latter context, they should be called *domains*). For example, the conceptual and perceptual domains are parts of the subjective domain, which is in turn a part of the physical universe.

Each of these three different universes can serve as a point of view; a reference point from which to view things, and which is composed of references to other universes.

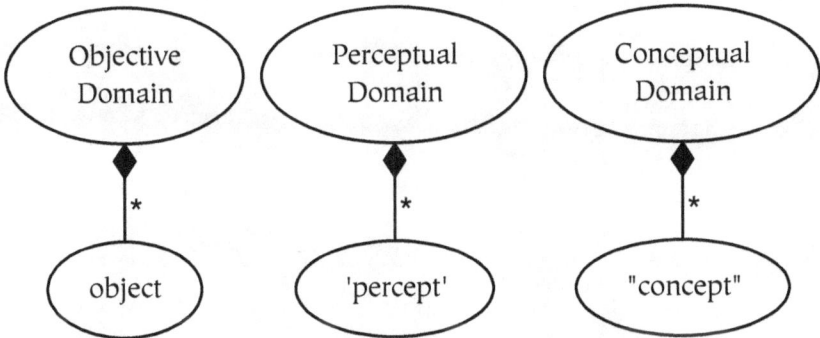

Chapter 4: The Physical Universe

All things are parts of the physical universe.

The physical universe includes every thing, in both this and every other world, from the physical (non-referential) point of view. It occupies the full range of every dimension which is attributed to it, including the temporal. Implied in this statement is that even mental phenomena are physical, in addition to whatever else they may be.

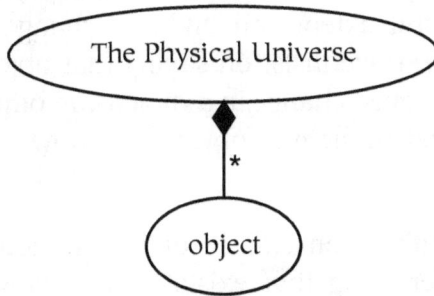

4.1: Dimensions of the Physical Universe

The dimensions most commonly attributed to the physical world are the three spatial and the temporal.

If the parts of a universe have a dimensionality equal to the universe that contains them, then clearly the dimensionality of a universe has direct consequences for all of the objects which it contains. For example, if space is defined as a four-dimensional entity, then objects must also be four-dimensional entities (i.e. they must contain their temporal extent). This entails that four-dimensional things are not alterable (or mutable): only objects *without* a temporal extent can undergo change (or vary as a function of time). If we insist on saying that objects do change, then at least they must change in a dimension other than the four which serve to define them as objects. So: how do we define the universe?

Many people, either consciously or unconsciously, define the universe as "everything that exists". Note, however, that this definition can be somewhat misleading for at least two reasons:

1. Everything is often taken to imply only matter, or every material thing, in which case *empty space* is left out of (or somehow in between) the concept of the universe. This empty space should be included in the concept of everything, so that there is nothing that is not included in our concept of everything (i.e. "empty space" is something, however nebulous, even if it is just the relationship between objects).

2. "Everything that exists" connotes only the present moment. As such, it cannot contain objects which have a temporal extent (as opposed to objects that exist only in the present). Although it is tempting to say that the physical world is everything that currently exists, the notion of *what is current* turns out to be

a matter of perspective (according to most current physical theories).

An alternative definition of the physical universe is an entity or event which occupies all possible values of all dimensions upon which it is described.[1] This corrects the two shortcomings of the previous definition, both of which are due to their failure to occupy the full extent of some dimension. In the first case, the notion that the universe is material carries the implication that the universe only exists where material exists. In the second case, a universe that exists only at one time (even though it occupies all three spatial dimensions) cannot contain the universe as it is witnessed by multiple observers. A complete universe, by contrast, exists in every part of every dimension. The universe is that thing of which every other thing is a part, where both spatial and temporal parts are considered.

How many dimensions does the universe have? Historically, the world has been described with three spatial dimensions. The temporal dimension was added to these three spatial dimensions relatively recently: time is now commonly known as the fourth dimension (at least to physicists, to whom it is the fourth dimension in a particular type of four-dimensional space called Minkowski space).

Four-dimensional space, or four-space, is required to describe the universe because the simultaneity of events depends on the observer (or the observer's frame of reference). In other words, the order of events (i.e. which events happen at the same time) is not the same for all observers, as would be the case if there were a *simultaneous space* for all observers. The Euclidean conception of a single extended spatial entity that exists at a single time is physically untenable: there is no single *time* for all positions, or all observers.

There is a certain amount of circularity, of course, in arguing that the universe has a certain number of dimensions because that is how many are needed in our symbolic formulation of its physical laws. For one thing, this argument ignores that the physical laws could be expressed in different ways. For example, we could express a two-dimensional coordinate using two real numbers and a Euclidean coordinate system, such as the point at [y=1 inch, x=1 inch]. The same point in space, however, could be located in a number of different ways: using polar coordinates, it could be specified as [angle=45 degrees, radius=1.414 inches]. That point could also be described using a single complex number as [1 + i]. All of these formulations have two coordinates, but the coordinate system (or the set of basis vectors) that is used to locate the point is different.

In general, although some number of coordinates may be required, we can choose any dimensions (or basis vectors) that we like. Similarly, although the equations that express Einstein's principles of relativity are easily expressed in Minkowski space, they could be expressed in any number of spaces. To say that the universe has a certain number of dimensions because it gives a convenient formulation for spacetime equations is to make the argument that it will be convenient if we talk about things this way, as opposed to saying that things have a particular dimensionality and can have no other. According to this nominalistic argument, theories of physics which use ten or more dimensions in their equations (such as various kinds of string theory) provide evidence for the universe having a similarly high dimensionality. Similarly, theories of physics with fewer than three spatial dimensions are possible, although it makes the mathematics more difficult. Flatland is an example story about such a world.[2]

In a nutshell, it seems that when events are described in the physical universe, a high number of dimensions (at least higher than three) are necessary to locate them.[3] However, it seems reasonable to assert that the primitive of the physical universe is at least a four-dimensional thing, or an event, as opposed to a substance which undergoes actions (i.e. things in three-space to which we add a temporal dimension). These high-dimensional things, which are non-referential parts of the physical universe, are called objects.

The Nature of the Physical Dimensions

The physical dimensions are most often conceived to be Euclidean.

What is the nature of the physical dimensions? For example, are they circular, or do they extend infinitely in a given direction? Are they orthogonal (at right angles) to one another? Are they infinitely divisible (or continuous)?

Most of us are at least implicitly committed to some idea of the structure of the dimensions of the physical universe. Probably the most common mental model of the dimensions of the physical universe, at least in the western world, are Euclidean dimensions. To say that dimensions are Euclidean is approximately equivalent to saying that given an arbitrarily assigned origin, the dimensions extend to infinity in orthogonal directions. In other words, physical space can be measured by numbered axes which form right angles to one another. However, this understanding of dimensionality is certainly not the only possibility.

One alternative to Euclidean dimensions are circular dimensions (or in the N-dimensional case, hyperspherical dimensions). For example, imagine that you are an ant traveling on the surface of a sphere: if you go far enough in a given direction, even though you are traveling in a straight line with respect to the surface, you will come back around to where you started.[4] This notion of dimensionality does not require infinite extent, and also avoids a number of problems associated with finite dimensions. For example, suppose that the spatial dimensions are finite, and that there is a boundary beyond which one cannot go. This scenario is difficult to comprehend: if there was a boundary, then what happens when an object crosses it? Does the boundary move? In which case, in what sense was it a boundary?

As opposed to this somewhat paradoxical notion of a spatial boundary, holding a corresponding belief in a finite temporal boundary is relatively popular: a large number of people believe in a moment of creation and a moment of destruction (these two beliefs often, but not always, go together). Westerners often understand the temporal dimension to be a linear quantity which extends (possibly "infinitely") in both directions. The Hopi, a native American tribe, see time as circular; the Vedic tradition of India also envisions epochs of time as recurring. Physicists talk of the beginning of time (the big bang), and sometimes of its end (the big collapse).

These differing points of view indicate that the dimensions have a nature which is uncertain, precisely because that nature has been viewed with relative certainty in a number of different ways. We can paraphrase this disconnect by saying that the physical dimensions which we use to describe the world have certain properties which are characteristic of our description. At least to some extent, space and time are conceptual contraptions: they are the basis vectors by which we measure objects in space.

4.2: Parts of the Physical Universe

The parts of the physical universe are called objects.

Parts of the physical universe share the dimensionality of the physical universe, even if they are atomic (although atoms have only unit measure in each dimension). For example, parts of a four dimensional universe must be four dimensional entities. The parts of the physical universe are called *objects*: since the universe is considered to be (at least) four-dimensional, another word for these objects might be *events* (where it is implied that the events have a nonzero duration). The physical universe contains all of us as objects: we are each a part of it. Since from a physical perspective our minds are our brains, they too are a part of the universe. Therefore, parts of perception (percepts) and parts of conception (concepts) are kinds of objects, at least when they are understood non-referentially. This is represented in the following figure:

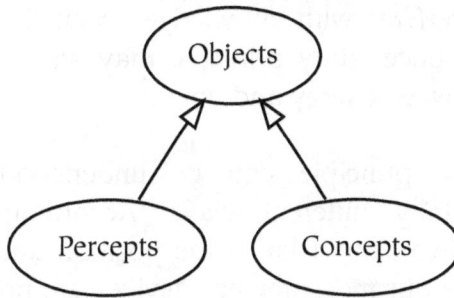

Primitives of Reality:
Spatial Things versus Events

All objects occupy a nonzero interval of time.

What are the primitives of reality? Are there things out of which reality is composed, such that there is a unique decomposition into these things? Both conceptually and physically, it seems unlikely that there is a unique decomposition; the world may be partitioned in numerous different ways. However, is it possible to at least characterize which *types* of things constitute valid parts? For example, things can be described as either spatial things which endure through time, or as things which have an inherent temporal aspect. In other words, are things three-dimensional, and do we perceive most of them, or are they four-dimensional, and of them do we perceive only a slice?[5] To address this question we look at several findings from modern physics.

One of the more interesting findings from physics is that when one attempts to measure a physical object, a trade-off is encountered between knowledge of its position (the spatial location) and knowledge of its momentum (which is the velocity of an object in a given direction multiplied by its mass). According to quantum physics, the product of the standard deviation of these two quantities two cannot be less than a particular constant value. This law, known as Heisenberg's Uncertainty Principle, states that knowledge of one measurement entails imprecise knowledge of the other measurement; knowledge about the position interferes with knowledge about the velocity, and vice-versa (the uncertainty principle may also be stated as a relationship between energy and time).[6]

The uncertainty principle can be understood in at least two fundamentally different ways. According to the first understanding, we cannot know the position and velocity of a particle because our measurement devices are not sufficient. In other words, there is a definite position and velocity, but we cannot measure it. According to the second understanding, there *is* no definite position and velocity to be measured. In other words, we cannot know these quantities because they do not exist as definite properties of the object. The latter interpretation of quantum mechanics, called the Copenhagen interpretation, is the more popular of the two. In this interpretation, the position and momentum of the object do not exist as precise entities to be quantified in the first place.

Other interesting findings from quantum physics that challenge our assumptions about reality revolve around something called the particle-wave duality. The particle-wave duality refers to the fact that small things such as photons, the particles which constitute light, behave like both waves and particles. When photons impact a surface such as a photographic sheet, we observe them as points: they impact in a very definite location. However, when photons travel through space, they exist as waves.

The particle-wave duality is illustrated in a famous study called the double slit experiment. In that experiment, photons are shot from a source, pass through either one or two narrow openings (slits), and eventually impact upon a photographic plate. In both cases, at the time of impact, the photons act like particles which leave their mark in a well-defined location. When a single slit is open, the pattern of impact on the plate is a normal density, centered on the slit (i.e. there is a Gaussian distribution around the bullseye). However, when two slits are open, there are not two normally-distributed impact patterns as one would expect. In fact, the photographic plate displays an interference pattern; a photon acts as if it goes through both slits, and subsequently interferes with itself. This is not problematic for a wave-like thing, which is distributed in space, but a wave-like thing would not impact the photographic plate in a single point. It is problematic for a point-like thing, since one would expect that the point would go through one slit or the other, and therefore not both (which is necessary to cause an interference pattern). This incongruous behavior is an example of the phenomena called particle-wave duality.

Despite this incongruous behavior, there is a very accurate model of the behavior of the photon which relies on what are called Schrodinger's wave equations. In contrast to the wide acceptance of these equations, however, the interpretation of the phenomena these equations characterize is widely debated. According to the Copenhagen interpretation, the photon travels through both slits as a "probability wave". That probability wave *collapses* when it is measured, for example when it hits the photographic plate, and one of the probabilities actualizes. In terms of the equation, this collapse involves setting some number of variables to zero that govern the probabilistic behavior, which coincides with the point-like nature of the particle at that instant. The wave-like nature is explained by saying that the particle exists as a cloud of possibilities, and these possibilities interfere with one another to create the pattern. Of course, this interpretation introduces the need for a theory that explains when and why probability waves collapse, which is where this theory gets particularly controversial.[7] In another theory called the multiple-worlds interpretation, the wave functions do not collapse at all: the multiple alternatives *all* actualize, each in different physical universes (the universes are said to *branch* at that instant).

Perhaps one way of accounting for these phenomena is to say that particles are in fact things of high dimensionality (instead of things which are limited to three dimensions). For example, if we consider particles to occupy a region in both space and time, then they would appear like curve segments in spacetime (where the length of the curve corresponds to the relative velocity of the particle). In order to occupy a single location in space, the particle would have to remain immobile for an amount of time greater or equal to its temporal extent (otherwise its location at the beginning would not occupy the same spatial position as its position at the end). Similarly, if a particle is not moving, it is impossible to determine its directionality (and thus its momentum, because it has no temporal orientation). In any case, these are speculations based on the assumption that objects are four-dimensional. If we further assume that objects are five-dimensional, then understanding particles as probability-waves falls out rather naturally (recall the earlier chapter in which the fifth dimension was equated with possibility).[8]

Regardless of one's interpretation of these phenomena, it seems clear that our everyday understanding of physics falters when presented with the evidence gathered from these experiments. However, our misunderstanding in this case may be telling: it may shed light on the nature of our cognition if we can understand why we had this mistaken understanding. One possible answer to this question has to do with the relation between the physical and perceptual universes. In particular, if we suppose that the perceptual universe was a reduced-dimensionality representation of the physical universe, then to base our conception of reality on perception would lead to exactly such an incorrect conclusion.

In that case, this lost dimensionality could be recovered, but it would take a good deal of conceptual work.

4.3: The Subjective/ Objective Dichotomy

The division between the subjective and the objective defines life.

Our experience is subjective because we observe it. Through experience, we learn about a world which is independent of the subjective world, in which objects persist independently of our observation of them: the objective world. This distinction is incredibly significant; it is certainly one of the first distinctions we learn. This book follows an inverted development in this respect: it begins with the physical universe, and then proceeds to examine the subjective universe.

It is not possible to resolve which of the subjective or physical universes ultimately contains the other. Saying that the subjective domain is a part of the physical universe, and that the physical universe is more than the combination of all of the subjective universes, implies that the objective domain exists independently of our perception of it. This characterization of things amounts to the claim that "if a tree were to fall in the woods and no one were there to hear it, it would still make a sound". Although this point of view is widely accepted, it is not *necessarily* true: the strongest claim that any of us can make on the basis of our experience is that a tree falling makes a sound if we hear it (or otherwise measure it).[9]

An apple has properties that we cannot directly perceive, such as chemical bonds, electromagnetic forces, etc. Among the properties of the apple that we can perceive, such as the exterior of the apple, we only see aspects of the side that faces us. The distinction between what we can and cannot observe, is the distinction between the subjective and the objective domains. The subjective universe is a high-dimensional thing that consists of all the things that we perceive in our lifetime, and encompasses inner phenomena such as thought. Although we are often not aware of all of our neuronal processing, it is still a part of the subjective domain (although we may not always pay attention to it).

Although it is misleading to define a sharply demarcated line between the subjective and objective domains, we will (somewhat arbitrarily) make the claim that the border between the subjective and the objective domains is the border of the nervous system (which is taken to include both the central and the peripheral nervous systems). Note that this border is established from the objective point of view: from the subjective point of view, there are no borders (i.e. it is not possible for an individual to perceive the edge of their nervous system).

4.3.1: The Objective Domain

The objective domain consists of those things which are not referential.

By social convention and experience, we establish that there are things which are not directly perceived, but that are still present. These things are collectively known as the objective domain. The hair on the back of our head, assuming that we do not perceive or otherwise sense it, is a part of the objective domain (i.e. something is not subjective only in virtue of being a part of our body). Again, a thing is a part of the subjective domain in virtue of the fact that we perceive it. Hence, the hair on the back of someone else's head may be a part of our subjective domain.

This fact illustrates that the subjective/objective dichotomy is different than the dichotomy between self/other. The self is an organism whose boundary is determined from the outside, but the subjective universe is determined by the perception of that organism (i.e. from the inside). Again, note that the subjective universe does not exhibit a boundary when viewed from the inside; by merely looking at two hands, one of which is mine and one which is yours, there is no *necessary* reason to assign the label "mine" to one of them (based on immediate perceptual evidence, and neglecting sight of the arm that connects to a body). Of course, I have physical sensation of my hand that I do not have of yours, but I do not have physical sensation of my hair, and that is still typically considered a part of my self.

One of the primary distinguishing characteristics of living things, which are the containers of subjective universes, is the ability to move about. Our ability to move our body is important for both the formation of one's self-concept as well as the determination of other objects as animals. Therefore, the next section briefly examines several externally observable differences between the living and the lifeless.

Causation

The actions of lifeless things are determined from the outside.

An object is affected by gravity in virtue of its mass. Expressed slightly differently, there is a property called mass in virtue of which one can determine the action of the object. A rock is going to fall to the earth with a certain inertia in virtue of its mass. In this case, the rock's mechanism of action is so obvious (or transparent) that we might even say that the rock has nothing to do with it. This mechanism is in stark contrast to the mechanism behind the action of animals, which often have extensive brains and complicated (or at least opaque) mechanisms of action. A snake slithers toward food in virtue of various muscular and neural machinery. Owing to this machinery, the motion of a snake takes into account the world as that world has been experienced over the snake's lifetime (as opposed to the motion of a rock, whose wellsprings of action are a good deal more immediate).

The extent to which the immediate external causes of a thing determine its mechanism of action is the extent to which that thing is not self-determined. Self-determination often entails having the intrinsic properties of unpredictability and intelligence (the latter is necessary to rule out pure randomness). Because animals have some internal complexity or memory in virtue of which they act, animals are *free* (as opposed to being controlled directly by external forces). The cause of the action of an animal or otherwise independent entity comes largely from within, even if that within has ultimately come from without.

As an example of causation, if the wind rustles in an apple tree, and a branch shakes, and an apple falls on my head, one might say that the wind *caused* the apple to fall. Not only did one thing happen before the other, but the earlier thing *made* the latter thing happen. As a result, the later thing was unavoidable; the cause required the effect to occur. In this understanding, the future is uniquely determined by the present; it is simply waiting to unfold. Before the effect (the apple falling), the cause (the wind blowing) is present; that cause, in turn, can be seen as the effect of yet another cause (perhaps the low pressure system in the area).[10]

There are several things to consider about the mental model behind this causal description of the falling apple. The rustling wind, at an earlier time, consisted of bits of matter and energy which were dispersed throughout the world: when all the causes and conditions come together in the right way, the tree is shaken, and the apple falls. One implication of this description is the *billiard-ball* model of causation. Despite the fact that the wind is dispersed, the billiard-ball model implies that one thing causes another thing, which causes yet another thing. This view of things is rigid in that it presupposes a unique decomposition of space into objects, and then implies that one event is the unique (or at least the primary) cause of the next event in the causal chain. However, there is no *unique* decomposition of reality into things, and even if there were, many (if not all) of those things contribute to any given effect. The apple would not have fallen unless the stem was weak, and gravity was present, and any number of other causal factors all came together to contribute to the result.

If we accept that animals are determined, we may describe their behavior with a deterministic language: they do certain things because from one point of view, those things were inescapable. In this case, however, we must also accept that they exist in a multi-faceted causal context, where part of their determination is internal and part is external. This means that we can still use the language of volition: in fact, it means that the language of volition is applicable to a larger class of objects, just as is the language of determination. In essence, if *free* means caused from within and *determined* means caused from without, then the boundary between freedom and determination becomes merely a spatial boundary. Applying the language of volition to inanimate objects, we might say that a rock *decides* its future course of action in virtue of its mass. A radioactive rock will cause clicking on a Geiger counter in virtue of its radioactivity. Of course, the rock always makes the same decisions: it is not all of a sudden bestowed with lots of creativity. It does not engage in a thinking process: that is in part what makes it a rock, instead of a person. Subjectively, though, this kind of talk can transfer a feeling-tone to inanimate objects which was previously reserved for animate objects. It can also help us to feel mercy for people who make stupid decisions. Of course, all of this is an uncommon use of language: we are stretching the boundaries of what we generally mean by a free decision. But to some extent, that is exactly what the debate of free will and determinism is all about.[11]

4.3.2: The Subjective Domain

The subjective domain consists of those things which, for some individual, refer to things in the physical universe.

As discussed in the previous section, which objects are alive can be partly assessed based on the internality of their causes.

Universes

However, it feels odd from a subjective point of view to say that we are caused: we prefer to say that we are free to do as we like. This section looks a bit more closely at causation from a subjective point of view, or individual volition, in light of the fact that physics seems deterministic.

The Source of Volition

Living things are described as having a choice.

Many people believe that their fate is escapable: hence, they apply the language of causation to inanimate objects. As for themselves, they are *free* to do whatever they decide to do. In fact, determinism admits that people are free to do whatever they decide to do. Further, people are free to decide what they decide to do. In light of this, even determinism is quite free. What determinism disallows, however, is that people that came into being can recursively choose what they decide, in a way that begs an infinite regress. According to Schopenhauer, "A man can surely do what he wills to do, but he cannot determine what he wills".

If living beings are completely free in the sense that they can determine both their current choices *and* all the causes that led to that determination, then the implied infinite causal regress necessitates that these beings have always existed. In other words, if they are their own cause, then they must already have existed in order to determine their subsequent choice (assuming that they did not come into existence causelessly), and in this process it seems that there could be no first moment (as they would not have been around in the prior moment in order to cause themselves). On the other hand, if individuals are born from causes and conditions other than themselves, then they are determined (at least originally) by that which is other than themselves.

It is probably not a coincidence that people who maintain the existence of ultimate individual freedom often hold that a soul entered the body from somewhere else, and that this soul has existed forever. Pre-existing selves, which have existed forever, allows ultimate freedom to be maintained even though bodies are created in the context of a deterministic world.

Many people have gone to great lengths to deny causality: some individuals try to avoid this argument by saying that freedom is a form of randomness. Whether or not it is possible to be truly random, it is quite possible to have numerous causes instead of just a few, which would lead to complex (if not truly random) behavior. However, true randomness as a source of action is probably not enormously satisfying, because even though we are no longer *determined*, our freedom to do things becomes entirely random: although we win freedom from determination, we simultaneously strip volition of any meaningful intent.

There is exactly one thing for which ultimate freedom is not a paradoxical notion: everything. Everything is *entirely* free, and is in no way unfree: it could not possibly be controlled or determined by something else, since there is no other thing whatsoever. Hence, just as the notion of everything depends on one's perspective, whether something is free or not depends on perspective. From an objective perspective, it may be impossible for a part to be free, since that part exists in a causal context. That part, however, may be an entire subjective perspective, and from that point of view it is a whole and could not possibly be determined by anything else. These two truths do not contradict one another: they are each valid from their own point of view. Considered as a part, a thing is determined by other parts: as a whole, a thing has nothing else by which it could be determined.

Notes

[1]This is a bit circular in that it begs the question of which dimensions are used to describe the universe. However, most axiomatic systems have a somewhat awkward beginning, and this definition is well-suited to a nominalistic viewpoint.

[2]Flatland is a two-dimensional world that was originally described in [Abbott]. Three dimensional people do enter that land, but they have unexplainable properties from the point of view of the Flatlanders.

[3]In fact, even if the dimensionality of the physical universe was less controversial, we would still be reluctant to accept it, since physical theories suffer from the unfortunate tendency to change rather often relative to the laws that they attempt to describe. We will not attempt to fix an upper limit to the number of dimensions; in practice, we use as many as are required in order to speak intelligibly about the world.

[4]This model of the spatial dimensions was proposed by Albert Einstein, among others.

[5]Four-dimensional objects are also called *occurrents* (see [Simons]).

[6]To put a linguistic spin on Heisenberg's Principle, we might say that the more we know about the object, or the more we characterize it as a noun, the less we can understand about its movement through time, or the less well we may characterize it with verbs. Of course this is a metaphor; Heisenberg's uncertainty principle is intended to apply only to small things in the physical universe, not to the conceptual universe. However, it is also true of the conceptual universe that one cannot exactly identify the noun (spatial position or description) without affecting the verbs (temporal position or description) that apply to an object: the more precisely a noun refers to (or restricts) its referent, the fewer verbs may be applied to that noun. To use a concrete example, if we describe an apple as having the quality of redness, then it becomes difficult to say that the apple ripens, since redness is a quality which changes through the process of ripening. In other words, by placing an increasing number of (spatial) constraints on the apple, the apple becomes less capable of undergoing transformation (without losing its identity).

[7]It is an interesting question what exactly it is that makes a probability wave collapse. Does it have to do with interactions between events, or does it have something to do with the act of observation? This question was formulated by Schrodinger in terms of knowing if a cat in box was alive or dead, but it seems to be the same conundrum as whether a tree falling in the woods makes a sound, even if no one is there to hear it.

[8]When a particle impacts a photographic plate, the space which it occupies along the fifth dimension contracts; physicists say that the probability wave *collapses* at this point. Given what we have said and will say about changes to the dimensionality of objects, however, we would expect that the probability wave never *entirely* collapses; even after impact, the photon would continue to occupy

a nonzero interval on the dimension of possibility, otherwise this would amount to a reduction in dimensionality.

[9]If you are someone who believes that there is no objective domain above and beyond the many subjective domains which we describe as being a part of it, feel free substitute the term "multi-subjective universe" for the term "physical universe", and assume that talk about the physical universe is talk about it as it is observed (or could be observed).

[10]This logic entails both that causes require effects and that effects require causes.

[11]Treating what was previously considered to be mental as material does not remove the mental aspect of things. In fact, if the language of volition applies to us, and we are material beings, then it makes sense to apply the language of mentality to other material things. This approximates a doctrine known as animism or panpsychism, which holds that all things have a psyche, or that all objects have a (limited) subjective experience as well as an objective one.

Chapter 5: The Subjective Universe

The subjective universe is the part of the physical universe that is directly perceived by a single individual.

Even though the subjective universe is a proper part of the physical universe, it is everything from a subjective point of view. For any subject, there is no going beyond it, and there is no perception of anything except it.

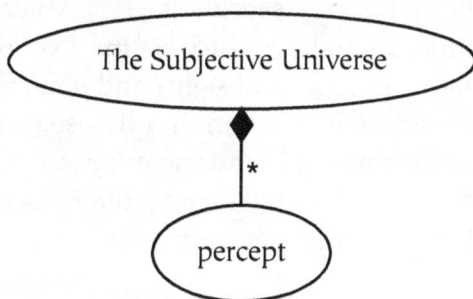

5.1: Dimensions of the Subjective Universe

The most common partition of the subjective universe involves five external and several internal senses, which together form a nominal dimension.

Each of us perceives different things. We perceive objects which others do not (in virtue of being in different locations), we perceive the same things differently (in virtue of our perceptive and mental faculties), and we perceive different inner experiences (perception of various emotions, feelings, sensations, etc). Much of perception can be divided into modalities, such as the five external senses (smell, taste, touch, hearing, and sight) and a number of internal senses (mental, emotional, and various other senses). Perception, as the term is used in this book, covers both perception of external reality and perception of internal reality: things such as memories, perception of the thought process, emotions, etc.

The scope of the term perception as it used here is somewhat broader than its scope when used elsewhere, in that it includes sensation. In certain other contexts, perception often refers only to the level of mental awareness in which multiple sensory modalities are united; the level at which the smell of an apple and the sight of an apple come together to form the percept 'apple', which is located somewhere in perceptual space. Although our use of the term perception includes the space in which percepts occur, it also includes the lower-level sensations. The difference between these is not relevant to our purposes here: what *is* relevant is the distinction between perception and conception. Although concepts can be perceived, they are also categorically different: they are referentially different.

In order to get a better understanding of subjective experience, it is useful to divide perception into parts. Perception is enabled by different modalities, namely the five external senses (smell, taste, touch, hearing, and sight) and several internal senses (which are categorized in various ways). We will refer to these types of perception as external perception and internal perception. External perception is the perception of things outside of the body, and internal perception is the perception of things originating within one's body (these are closely related to the notions of exteroception and interoception). To illustrate the matter graphically, we may divide subjective experience as follows:

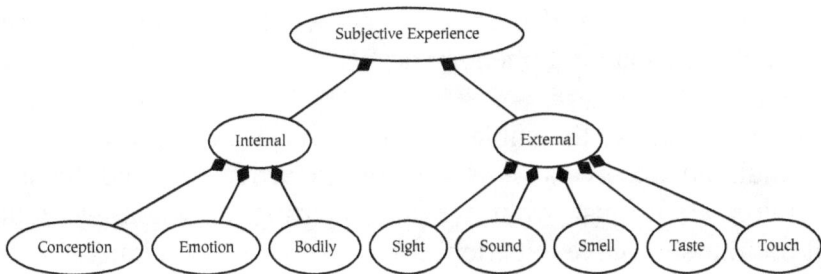

Figure 5.1: Senses

The five external senses are well known: by comparison, the internal senses are poorly known, or at least poorly communicated. Although internal sensations may be well known to individuals, they are difficult to talk about: the language describing internal sensation is difficult to precisely define. Language develops best for phenomena that can be directly observed by multiple speakers, since in that context the correct or incorrect application of words can be verified easily. Hence, the categorization of internal perception presented here is very crude: it is divided into conception, various emotions, and bodily sensations. These terms should be understood as an exhaustive categorization of internal phenomena (i.e. they divide internal perception into three parts *by definition*). For example, *thought* encompasses all rational mental events; emotion includes things like good and bad sensation, various kinds of pleasure and pain, and many others. Bodily perception (or bodily awareness) is therefore somewhat of a catch-all term: it encompasses proprioception, which means the perception of the location of one's body in space, as well as other internal percepts which are neither emotional nor conceptual.

Although the subjective universe has been divided here into eight parts, the most relevant division of the subjective universe in this book is perception/conception: hence, perception should be understood to contain external and most internal perception. Even emotions are viewed as things which are perceived, despite that the perception of them is phenomenally different than the perception of external phenomena.[1]

Precisely because the subjective domain does not present itself to multiple observers, it is difficult to arrive at a consensus opinion about just what we are referring to when we talk about our subjective experience. Perhaps one day a language of subjective experience will be developed which is highly correlated with the objective observation of physiological processes (i.e. a language that can be validated). In other words, physiological observation will serve as the basis for a language that describes our internal states (i.e. one which maps well onto our hormones, neurotransmitters, and various physiological structures).

External Perception

The dimensionality and mapping of the various sensory modalities is sense-specific.

Experience is processed according to its modality: the dimensions of each modality differ from one another. Within each modality, sensation is mapped from the outside of the organism to the inside: this mapping is mediated by neurons. This mapping only preserves certain relations, and the mapping itself is quite complex.

One way in which this complexity manifests is that certain areas of the external world are represented with more cortical area than others, which leads to a greater sensitivity (or selectivity). For example, our sensitivity to sound at high or low frequencies is lower than our sensitivity at the center of the audible range. The visual field is more sensitive to the intensity of light at the periphery than at the center. The sensation of touch is more acute at the fingers than at the forearms. In fact, the input which is received from the fingers, in terms of cortical size, is disproportional to the input from the forearm. Hence, we literally perceive *more* of our fingers than we do of our forearms: even though fingers occupy a smaller amount of physical space, they appear to occupy a larger amount of perceptual space (based on the amount of cortex used to represent them).

This mapping of the body to the cortex (or surface) of the brain has been studied extensively. In doing so, it has been observed that this mapping varies somewhat across individuals. Further, the cortical area corresponding to various areas of your physical body can change over time. For example, if you take piano lessons, the size of the cortical area that is dedicated to your fingers will increase.

To return to the topic of this section, an approximate (and certainly incomplete) attempt at characterizing the dimensions of the different external modalities is shown in the following table:

Sense	Dimensions
sound	pitch, timbre, volume
vision	position (up, down, left, right), color (RGB), brightness
taste	sweet, bitter, sour, salty and umami (the taste of monosodium glutamate)
touch	hard, soft, hot, cold, rough, smooth
smell	nice? stinky?

Table 5.1. The Dimensions of the Modalities

In the table above, most of the dimensions enumerated in the column on the right are merely illustrative, and somewhat arbitrary. The analysis of taste however, and in particular the taste receptor corresponding to the flavor *umami*, is the result of research by the scientist Kikunae Ikeda in 1908. There are five different known types of taste *receptors* (the neurons which are responsible for the detection of sensory events). In addition to the fact that taste is located in the mouth, each of those types of receptors can be represented as a dimension.

Since we experience such a plethora of tastes, the relative paucity of types of taste receptors may be surprising. Part of this can be explained by the fact that most foods we eat also have a distinctive mouth feel and a different smell (the sensation of smell is heavily intertwined with taste). It should be noted that it does not take very many orthogonal dimensions to produce a dense quantification of phenomena: adding new dimensions to existing spaces increases the size of these spaces exponentially. In particular, adding a novel dimension to a space multiplies the size of that space by the number of divisions that occur in the new dimension. For example, if we perceptually discriminate twenty different intervals along each of the five dimensions of taste (which grossly underestimates our capacity), then we would be capable of 20^5 possible perceptions, or over three million different tastes.[2]

Some of the features (or dimensions) in the table above may be the result of aggregating smaller-scale features. For example, rough and smooth may be aggregates of lower-level physical sensations: a single perceptual point may be incapable of being either rough or smooth on its own. This table represents a list of those dimensions of perception that are truly external, or those that come from outside of the organism (perceptions which are aggregates of other perceptions are regarded as internal). For example, this is the reason that depth is not listed as a dimension of vision: we have determined the dimensionality of visual sensation by measuring *close to the eyeballs*, and monocular vision does not produce the phenomenon of depth (at least without a number of simplifying assumptions). It is only when further along the neural pathways deeper in the brain that we find the input from each eye is combined, and a *disparity map* is formed to determine the distance of a given object. The bottom line is that the dimensions of perception are significantly different when determined proximal to the organs of perception as opposed to when they determined are observed further inside the brain. In this example, the dimensionality of vision increases as we follow perception from external sensation inwards.

Internal Perception

Internal perception is responsible for like and dislike.

There are a large number of internal senses for which language is rather poorly developed. For example, if I say that I am feeling a little "zippy" today, you may not know exactly what I mean by this: you cannot directly perceive the subjective experiences that coincide with my feeling of "zippiness". The situation is different for the perception of external things: if we both perceive the same object, then we do not need to rely on symbolic communication to learn the conceptual mapping. This is one of the issues that makes the determination of exactly which emotions exist (and the dimensionality of each) a difficult topic.

There are a number of basic internal percepts, which are categorized as feelings or emotions. Many of these emotions are bound up with concepts: for example, we like certain things and dislike other things. Liking conceptual things (i.e. having a positive valuation for certain concepts) entails that we have learned an association between some enjoyable perception (pleasure) and that conceptual thing (e.g. the concept of an apple). Similarly, disliking something may have its root in experienced pain. The sensations of liking and disliking clearly have a dimension of intensity, and probably several others, but a vague characterization is suitable here.[3]

If like and dislike are perceived, instead of conceived, then they occur in a perceptual space. If I am eating ice cream, that perceptual space is easy to localize: there is some sweetness in my mouth. Coupled with this sweetness is the perceptual (visceral) *like* of 'ice cream': although it may later be responsible for transferring a positive valuation to the *concept* of "ice cream", it is initially *perceptual* goodness. That perceptual goodness is not always easy to localize. For example, if you flirt with someone, it may be difficult to precisely localize the good feeling associated with that flirtation. On the other hand, this feeling certainly goes beyond purely conceptual happiness.

Although we claim that all percepts can be found within a perceptual space, they may not have a precise locality (perhaps this is related to the non-local effects of hormones and neurotransmitters). Even if internal senses are ultimately localizable, this location is often amorphous or hard to determine. For many people, however, internal perceptions are associated with particular areas of the body. Fear, for example, may occur in the belly; stress may occur in the shoulders. Although cognitive events may remain difficult to localize, most feelings are at least partially localizable, especially if we do not get too caught up in them.[4]

5.2: Parts of the Subjective Universe

All of our experience comes to us through our external and internal senses.

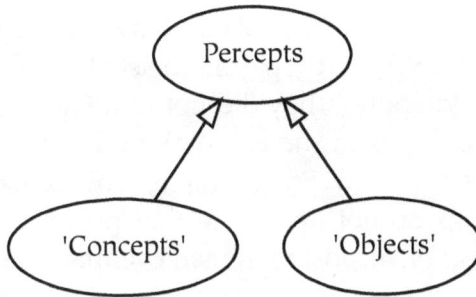

There is no way for us to perceive beyond the boundaries of our perception: to become aware of objects or concepts, they must be perceived. Although this is to some extent tautologous, it is worthwhile to consider that from the subjective point of view, objective reality is contained entirely in subjective experience, or the subjective universe.

The parts of the subjective universe are called percepts. Percepts are both things that we perceive as well as objects, in that our perception is mediated by the neurons of the brain. Of course, if a neurosurgeon were to look at the neurons responsible for our percepts, the neurons would not look to the neurosurgeon as they do to us. The electrical activity of the neurons firing are all that we have ever perceived, and for us, they do not fire randomly but in concert with the external world. In fact, from our perceptual point of view, they *are* the external world: we have a context for the neuronal activity that makes it meaningful. From the doctor's point of view, there is no such correlation: the doctor observes a small set of meaningless impulses.[5]

Perceptual Correspondence

Percepts are formed of both objects and concepts.

To form percepts that correspond to objects is just to perceive things. This act is so commonplace that we often forget that the objects are much richer in detail than the limited aspects of them that we perceive: we have an exaggerated expectation that things exist in the world in approximately the way that they appear to us. For example, when the early psychologists began looking inside peoples' heads (literally), they did not find internal mechanisms that looked like things in the external world: they found things of a very different nature. For example, when a person sees red things, red things do not appear in that person's head. On the one hand this is not surprising: to achieve this would be a rather remarkable feat of engineering. However, if the thing is not red in the brain, then what is it that is responsible for the subjective experience of red?

Although "red in reality" and "red in the brain" are quite different things, the perceptual mapping between these two is consistent: red things in reality produce a consistent effect in the brain, whatever effect that happens to be. This mapping also preserves several relationships between things in each domain: for vision, spatial relationships are preserved. So even though objects and percepts are quite different things, they have similar relationships to other things in their respective domains.[6]

As an example of the percept-object correspondence, imagine an apple as it is represented in both the physical universe and the perceptual universe. In the objective world, an enduring apple object can be seen as a collection of many instantaneous events. In the subjective world, an enduring apple concept can similarly be seen as a collection of many instantaneous events. For our concept of the "apple" to correspond to the apple object means that the apple events correspond to 'apple' percepts which are grouped together by an "apple" concept.

Our 'apple' percepts are very limited representations of the apple events; there are numerous properties of the object which are not represented. Of those features that *are* apparent, percepts are regarded to be very *direct*: they are expected to suffer from very little subjective distortion, and reflect reality as would a mirror.[7]

If a given percept corresponds well to a given object, we say that percept is valid; in other words, we correctly perceive the object. This contrasts with invalid percepts, such as hallucinations, for which there are no corresponding objects. Even if we hold that an apple does not exist in the world as a single object (i.e. any more than its two two half-apple parts), we still have a valid basis for calling the object an apple as opposed to an orange. In other words, even if our concepts do not physically resemble percepts, there are still reasons to apply the label "apple" as opposed to the label "orange".

Just as percepts can be of objects, they can also be of concepts (i.e. we can perceive concepts). Perceiving concepts, however, is a delicate art: it is all too easy to *conceive* of concepts, since that is most often their intended use: and that interferes with the *perception* of concepts. An example of forming percepts of symbols without additionally forming concepts that correspond to them occurs when listening to speakers of a language with which we are not familiar. In that case, although we are aware of the auditory sensations of the words (such as the pitch, volume, and timbre), we do not understand the meaning of the words.

Listening to speakers of a foreign language is by no means the only example of perceiving without conceiving: even in our native language, there are times when we listen to someone without understanding what they are saying. To some extent, our faculties of perception and cognition present us with a choice: perception of a thing and conception of that thing destructively interfere. The trade off between perception and conception applies not just to other people's speech, but to our own thought: to some extent, it is possible to be either perceivers or conceivers of our own thought process.

Spatial and Temporal Parts

Perception is perception of change.

All perception happens in the present. To some extent, this statement is tautologous due to the use of the present tense, which for most people implies existence at only a single point in time. The present is often conceived of as an interval of time so short that no change can take place. However, the present has also been called the *specious present,* in order to convey that it exists for a short duration of time (as opposed to existing at only a single instant).

We tend to perceive things that change: things that do not change are forgotten, even at a basic perceptual level. For example, if we eat sweet things all the time, then we adapt to this sweet baseline; it requires increasingly sweet stimuli to trigger the same sensation of sweetness. This acclimatization (or habituation) happens at the neural level, across all sensory modalities. Our perceptual functions are detectors of change: if the objects that we perceive do not change (relative to some baseline), then the percepts tend to disappear as our neurons grow accustomed to the stimulus.[8]

Vision is a particularly interesting modality for the study of habituation, since there is a physiological compensation for the habituation of the neurons: eye saccades. If you look at your environment without moving your eyeballs, your visual receptors habituate to it fairly quickly, and you will not see anything. We are prevented from encountering this situation in practice by eye saccades. Eye saccades are small, ubiquitous eye movements which provide the visual neurons with novel input by moving the eyes rapidly back and forth. Hence, each neuron sees change even in an unmoving scene: saccades generate change for our receptors to witness. We don't see the world similarly jerking about, because our higher-order perceptual processes counteract for the movement of the eyes.[9]

Attention

Awareness may be restricted to parts of certain dimensions.

Attention is an operation which restricts the domain of perception. The technical definition of the term attention is somewhat ambiguous (although it is better defined than the term consciousness). The term attention is used here to mean the restriction of perception, from an awareness of *everything* to an awareness of *something*. It is analogous to putting blinders on a horse: although it causes them to be less distracted, they are literally perceiving less. Visually, attention is related to the selection of a visual area. Linguistically, it is related to defining a universe of discourse. Mereologically, it is related to the selection of a universe from which parts are chosen. Although all of these mechanisms are not necessarily the same, the effects are similar.

The perceptual creation of a part out of a larger whole is analogous to the separation of a figure and its ground. The figure/ground dichotomy is borrowed from Gestalt psychology. In that system, the figure is the thing toward which attention is directed; it is more salient than the ground (and perhaps more important). When figure and ground are created, therefore, the figure comes to the forefront: this is similar to the part/complement relationship.[10]

Attention is a mechanism which can be arbitrarily directed: hence, it can be arbitrarily complicated. However, there are a number of basic perceptual principles which guide attention. Several of these have been formulated into what are called Gestalt laws, or grouping principles.[11] Some of the most common Gestalt laws are:

- Law of Closure: Percepts which are similar to percepts that have been seen previously are completed (i.e. the differences between the current and the remembered percept are ignored).

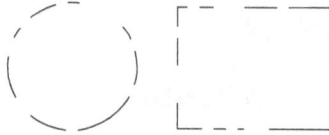

- Law of Similarity: Similar percepts (e.g. in terms of color, size, and various other properties) are grouped together.

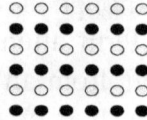

- Law of Proximity: Contiguous and continuous things are seen as the same thing.

- Law of Common Fate: Things moving in the same direction are perceived as the same thing (unfortunately, this is hard to represent in non-moving media).

5.3: The Conceptual/ Perceptual Dichotomy

A concept is a reference to a part of subjective experience, or a generalization of percepts.

There is a conceptual universe which consists of references to perception.[12] When understanding the conceptual universe, it is a universe with no boundaries; when perceiving it, it is a small part of the subjective universe (we perceive things other than concepts). Concepts are abstractions (or generalizations) of percepts, which live in a space with a radically different dimensionality than that of the things that they reference.

5.3.1: The Perceptual Domain

The perceptual domain is composed of perception: it includes sensation, excludes conception, and consists of references to objective reality.

If we hear someone speaking and we do not conceptually understand them, the utterance remains at the level of perception: the percepts do not become concepts. If we do understand them, concepts are activated, which potentially give rise to further concepts. This distinction between thought-as-perceived and thought-as-conceived lies at the root of a difference in the categorization of the senses which is exemplified by several eastern and western cultures. In western culture, perception is most often divided into five external parts and perhaps one or two internal senses, but cognition is left out (it operates on perception). In eastern cultures, cognition is often included in the domain of perception: it is something which is perceived. This difference in the relative position of conception is illustrated visually in the next two pictures.

In the following diagram, conception is represented as something which operates on perception (as opposed to something on which perception operates):

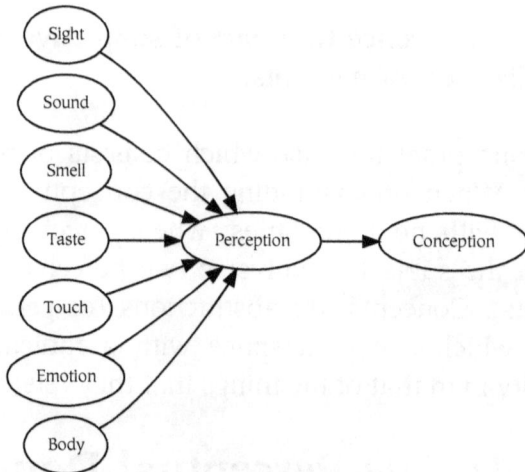

Figure 5.2: Western Sense Model

In this diagram, individual (external) senses are collected together into perception. Perception occurs at a location in which the senses are united in a perceptual space (these percepts are subsequently united in thought, as concepts). All perception, both external and internal, is spatial. This is immediately apparent for senses like sight, since they are instrumental in the formation of our spatial awareness in the first place. For example, everything in space that we see has a color, which occurs where the object with that color is present. It is also true of the internal senses: for example, taste occurs in the mouth, when we lick something.

In the following diagram, perception occupies the terminal position: concepts themselves are perceived, just as all other phenomena.

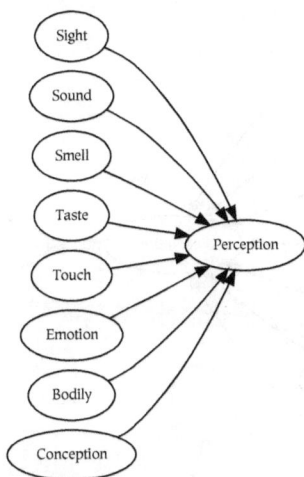

Figure 5.3: Eastern Sense Model

The rationale for introducing these two mental models is to set up an east-meets-west diagrammatic fusion. In the resulting mental model, conception is both something that is itself sensed as well as something that operates on data from other senses. As such, thinking is both something that can be perceived (as perceptual data) and conceived (as conceptual data).[13] Pictorially, information flows to and from the mental sense as follows:

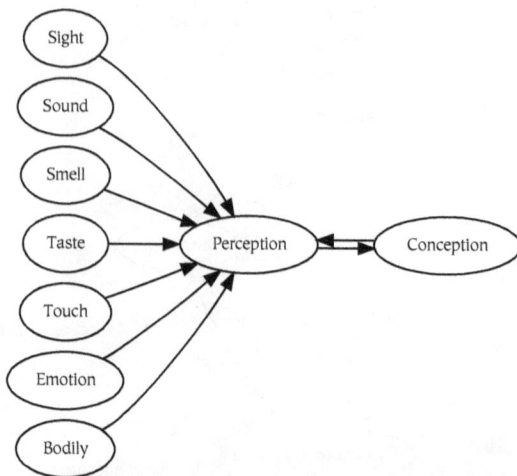

Figure 5.4: Combined Model of Sensation

This diagram is markedly dissimilar from the previous two diagrams in that it contains a feedback loop. This loop is analyzed in detail in Chapter 9,*Conceptual/Conceptual References.*

5.3.2: The Conceptual Domain

The conceptual domain is composed of things called concepts, which are references to percepts.

Concepts are things that are able to categorize the perceptual domain; exactly how they categorize that domain is driven by the desires of the organism.

A concept is often defined in one of two ways: either as a prototype or a collection. If a concept is defined as a prototype, then it is in some sense the *perfect example* of the category it represents. In this case, things are apples to the degree that they are similar to a single prototypical "apple" concept. If a concept is defined as a collection, then it represents a (potentially large) number of prototypes. In this case, however, there is not necessarily a single prototype that best represents the concept.

Prototypes and collections both serve to define concepts: these correspond to conceptual and perceptual definitions. While concepts may be formed by collecting other concepts, they are still ultimately reducible to functions operating on perception. In contrast to either of these two definitions, the perspective that we wish to emphasize is that a concept represents a dichotomy: we cannot create the concept "bird" without at the same time dividing the universe (or some restricted domain thereof) into bird and non-bird things.

Definition of a Concept

Concepts are categories of percepts which are the result of partitioning something.

Given a domain of discourse, a *concept* is defined as a proposition which selects some part of that domain. This proposition creates a decision boundary which partitions the input space: in other words, given a particular domain, a concept (which may or may not be associated with a given name) is associated with one of two ranges formed by the partition of the domain.

Each concept acts on its given domain as a function which forms a binary partition: such functions are called propositional functions, or simply propositions. In general, propositions should be understood as a function that can result in truth, falsity, or some value in between. As a simple example of a proposition, consider *isAnApple(x)*, which yields a value indicating whether certain percepts indicate the presence of an apple. This proposition, since it identifies or recognizes a given object with a range of values in between true and false, might properly be called a fuzzy proposition (fuzzy logic is the extension of classical logic to multivalued truth functions).

Despite the utility of fuzzy properties, concepts are notoriously binary-valued. Although being binary valued is not a necessary feature of concepts, it is certainly quite common. People who are highly conceptual seem particularly prone to this sort of black-and-white thinking. This unnecessary polarity may be due to the fact that concepts, even if they are only somewhat true or false, exclude other concepts from being conceived at the same time. In other words, even if a concept is not binary valued, it may result in categorical thinking in virtue of the fact that it presupposes one point of view as opposed to another.

Notes

[1]Although perception is a bit of an awkward word choice, the alternative of inventing a new word that denotes all experienced phenomena other than concepts seems worse. The fact that no such word already exists might be regarded as evidence that terminology in the subjective domain tends to be poorly developed.

[2]Because of this combinatorial explosion, modeling systems with many dimensions is a problem referred to in engineering circles as *the curse of dimensionality* (of course, this dimensionality is not a curse when it is time for dessert).

[3]The dichotomy of like/dislike is potentially coincident with those of pleasure/pain, happiness/sadness, attraction/aversion, want/don't-want, or desire/repulsion. These dichotomies all have slightly different meanings to different people, and we really intend a bit of all of them when we are talking about like/dislike.

[4]In fact, whole systems have been developed with the aim of localizing various bodily energies, the most famous of which is probably the Indian chakra system.

[5]Perceptual mappings near the exterior of the nervous system will have a close accord with the external world. For example, the optic nerve projects the visual field to our brains with such fidelity that if the neurosurgeon were to see the pattern of neural activity on the back of our brains, they could determine what we were observing. For example, in an experiment in which an fMRI scanned the back of the occipital lobe as the subject looked at various words (where the visual field is projected by the optical nerve), the words that the subject is looking at are clearly legible (i.e. the are projected onto the back of the brain with good fidelity). Yoichi Miyawaki et al, Visual Image Reconstruction from Human Brain Activity using a Combination of Multiscale Local Image Decoders, Neuron, December 10 2008

[6]The relationship between "red in reality" and "red in the brain" is known in philosophical circles as the problem of *qualia*.

[7]Upon a little reflection, the notion that perception reflects reality *without distortion* is a bit preposterous. Reality is relayed to us through electrical impulses, but the world consists of things which look different than lightning storms. There certainly is a mapping between these different domains, but they remain very different domains. Although we tend to agree with each other about what we observe, that does not make what we each observe identical to objects themselves.

[8]Is it meaningful to say that all perception is the perception of change? This speculation corresponds to the fact that the objects that we perceive are not objects without a duration, but rather objects-undergoing-change. Mathematically, this amounts to saying that we perceive object differences (i.e. finite differences) rather than objects themselves.

[9]Another example of the mind's ability to adapt to changes in perception is its ability to remap distorted perceptual fields. Examples of this come from

experiments in which subjects were forced to wear glasses that turned their worlds upside-down. It takes subjects only a few days to adjust to this change; in fact, taking off the glasses at the end of the experiment feels strange. These experiments were first conducted by George Stratton in the 1890s.

[10]It is not necessary to pay attention to the figure and neglect the ground, although we often do just that. This is not surprising, though, given that some increased level of relevance was what directed us to create the separation in the first place. To indicate the importance of both parts (i.e. the figure and the ground without that figure), and to underscore the fact that it is not possible to create just one part out of a larger whole, we emphasize *the division* between a part and its complement.

[11]Similar rules were formulated by Aristotle in terms of the associations between objects. However, since relations between objects often define the objects themselves, there is a large amount of overlap. Aristotle proposed the following four laws that influence whether things are associated:

- The law of contiguity: things which are close together in space and time.

- The law of frequency: things which co-occur, or happen at the same time.

- The law of similarity: things which are similar, or close together on some dimension.

- The law of contrast: things which are dissimilar, or far apart on some dimension.

[12]For Aristotle, perceptions were united in what he called the "common sense". The common sense unites the various subjective perceptions of the apple (i.e. the sight, smell, and taste). This book refers to these united things as concepts, and to the universe in which they live as the conceptual universe.

[13]This model is not a completely novel addition to either eastern or western thought: it is a combination of different emphases.

Chapter 6: The Conceptual Universe

The conceptual universe is the domain of language.

This chapter examines the conceptual universe. Unfortunately, concepts are difficult to study directly, and the reliability of self-report is a contentious issue. However, because we assume that language and thought are closely related, we are able to consider the manipulation of concepts in terms of their stand-ins: symbols.

The conceptual universe is everything from the conceptual point of view. Through conceptualization and naming, we *think*: we use the semantics of individual words, which are combined through the use of syntax. In virtue of the relation of these concepts to prior experiences, these concepts mean something.

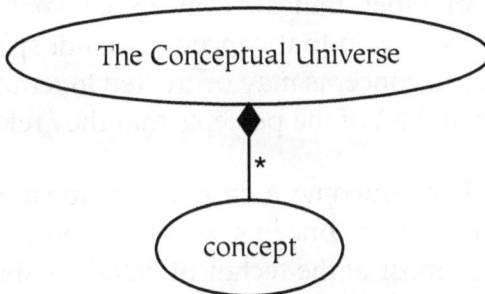

6.1: Dimensions of the Conceptual Universe

First-order concepts refer to percepts, which refer to objects; they derive their semantic value [meaning] from that which they reference and their relationship to other references.

There are numerous dimensions to the conceptual universe. Of key significance are the first conceptual dimensions to be formed; their study tells us a great deal about cognition because there are few complexities to deal with (at least when compared to the study of language use in adults).

Conceptual space is discrete: in other words, concepts are atomic. However, since concepts can be formed out of other concepts, there is a sense in which this is not the case (atomic things cannot be composed of other things). Conceptual space is different than perceptual space, in that concepts are not spatial. In some contexts, however, concepts may be treated in terms of the space (or the dimensionality) of the percepts that they reference.

This book has been building a case for the identification of the psychological notion of concepts with the mathematical notion of sets. Although most of the technical details of this association are left to the last section of the book, several basic similarities are worth pointing out. One is that sets and concepts can be both atomic and composed of other things. In other words, sets are singular entities, even though they may be composed of multiple entities: set braces have the power to unify that which they contain. Concepts have exactly that same quality: they are single entities themselves (which makes them atomic), although they may be defined as a collection of other things (which makes them non-atomic). In psychology, concepts are also known as generalizations or unitizations (behavioral psychologists in particular avoid associating with the word "concept", since its definition is often imprecise). The dual nature of both concepts and sets is understood in this book primarily in terms of reference: references themselves are singular, however they may refer to multiple entities in the referenced domain.

Decision Boundaries

Concepts unify the perceptual data on one side of a decision boundary.

A percept represents one side of a (perceptual) decision boundary. A concept, as it represents that percept either directly or indirectly, also entails a conceptual counterpart in virtue of its perceptual counterpart. This forms the basis of logical negation: if we know the concept of apple, we can form the concept of not-apple.

Without knowledge of the larger context in which a concept is defined, however, the logic of negation is somewhat illogical. This is made clear in a famous example by the philosopher Carl Hempel: "All ravens are black". First, note that this is a conjecture about objects (as opposed to being essential to the definition of a raven): it does not say that ravens are *necessarily* black. To make it clear that we are talking about the extensions of these concepts (i.e. actual ravens as opposed to the abstract concept of ravens), we might also say "the collection of all raven things is a part of the collection of all black things". In any case, because this statement is about the world instead of language, we cannot *necessarily* determine its truth or falsity. As we cannot know the truth conceptually (*a priori*), we must determine the answer in physical space (*a posteriori*).

Hempel asks which things constitute evidence for the statement that all ravens are black. It is not too difficult to see that every black raven that we encounter provides some amount of evidence for this statement. Hence, if we encounter a large number of ravens, we are led to believe in the universal applicability of

Hempel's statement. However, Hempel encourages us to consider an additional statement which is logically equivalent to "all ravens are black": "all non-black things are non-raven things".[1]

Given these features of inductive learning, however, every thing that we encounter which is a non-black non-raven adds evidence to the thesis that all non-black things are non-ravens, and therefore to the thesis that all ravens are black. However, this (logically equivalent) induction feels paradoxical for many people. It does not sit well with most people that a red bicycle adds support to the hypothesis that all ravens are black.

This finding may be partially explained by noting that the population of non-black non-ravens is much larger than the population of black ravens, so the support for the conclusion that is lent by examples from the larger population is limited to a similar extent. Non-raven things say relatively little about raven things, since the former set is so immense and diverse relative to the latter. However, if we imagine a small world in which only birds existed, encountering a non-black non-raven would provide more evidence for the hypothesis that "all ravens are black".

Intuition

A picture is worth a thousand words.

The discussion of the conceptual universe in this book focuses on its role in logical thought. However, direct analysis of concepts and thinking is difficult, in part because it relies on subjective report (where a large amount of subjectivity enters into the picture). Since language is easy to analyze relative to thought, and because of the strong correlation between them, this chapter focuses on words instead of directly on concepts. Unfortunately, there is at least one aspect of cognition which is unamenable to this treatment: intuition.

We take it for granted that studying the structure of languages can tell us a lot about the structure of thought. This assumption is related to a stronger, much-debated hypothesis, which is that conceptual thought is not significantly different than *mental speech*. Historically, theorists believing in this hypothesis (called the *Language of Thought* hypothesis) mapped what we knew about the operation of symbols directly onto the operating principles of the brain. This mapping produced biological models which were found to be largely untenable. However, to assume that the deep structure of a sentence corresponds to *some* internal (cognitive) representation of a thought seems undeniable.

Intuition is a kind of thinking which does not seem to be obviously perceptual or conceptual. Since intuition is so rich, it is tempting to associate it with perception as opposed to conception (since conception is often relatively dichotomous). However, intuition seems to be able to both use and transcend the limitations of the conceptual mind. So instead of classifying intuition as either rational or irrational, we classify intuition as multi-rational.

The way that syntax is used to combine words into sentences implies a single semantic hierarchy, as opposed to multiple hierarchies. In other words, although we might make a pun and thereby provide two or more conceptual hierarchies for a given sentence, the normal mode of (conceptual) understanding is to understand in only one way, or from one point of view. Intuition, by contrast, is a mass of connections and associations which are linked together in many ways. For the intuitive mind, everything is related to everything else.

When we intuit something, it is difficult to say how we arrived at that intuition: an intuition is too rich of a phenomenon to be described within the relatively narrow confines of several dozen symbols. Even though we cannot say exactly what an intuition is in a small number of words, it certainly is possible to say what is occurring in an individual who experiences an intuition: the subjective experience may not be able to be easily described, but it is possible to describe an intuition from an objective perspective. The experience is ineffable; its mechanism is effable.

An intuition is capable of grasping in an instant what it takes volumes of books to say. Again, it is multi-categorical, as opposed to noncategorical: it allows multitudes of associations to arise, as opposed to selecting only one or several. To categorize something is to make relevant a certain feature in virtue of which it is categorized; while that is certainly useful in some contexts, it simultaneously makes numerous other features of that object irrelevant. For example, an apple may belong to the thing-with-seeds category, but if we seize on this aspect of the apple too strongly, we will neglect its other aspects. If we bring only the seedy quality of the apple to the foreground, we forget that it is good to eat, or that it can be carved into tiny statues. For the apple-as-intuited, however, all things are relevant information. Intuition is capable of experiencing something in its entirety, at least in as far as that thing is known.

An intuited *something* is not either this or that: it is not something taken out of context, or understood in terms of its membership in only one or several categories: it is that thing as it relates to everything else. As a result, the expression of an intuition is a nontrivial task. This may account for the fact that intuitions are related to other intuitions, as opposed to being defined directly. These relationships are expressed as metaphor: for example, "Flesh is like grass" invites us to compare two concepts without being explicit about the numerous relations between them. There are countless implications and unstated associations in metaphor; so many that we rarely (if ever) enumerate all of them. So it stands to reason that we comprehend metaphor with intuition.

6.2: Parts of the Conceptual Universe

The parts of the conceptual universe are called concepts.

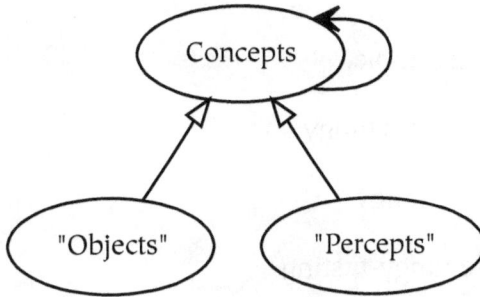

It is possible to think (or have concepts) about both the objective and the perceptual domains. Therefore, they are both parts of the conceptual universe. More precisely, references to them (or concepts of them) are parts of the conceptual universe. For example, consider the three phrases: "I am", "I perceive", "I think". To understand these phrases implies that their content (objects, percepts, and thoughts) is brought inside of the conceptual universe (as concepts which reference these things, of course, because only concepts can exist as such within the conceptual universe).

Sentences are singular references to events in the world. The top of the syntactic tree is typically a single concept which is a reference to the world (as opposed to being a reference to language). This single concept is created by the combination of other phrases, which may in turn be complete or incomplete concepts themselves. At the root of the tree, the primary syntactic division of the sentence creates a noun phrase and a verb phrase. These two phrases characterize the spatial and temporal dimensions of an N-dimensional object to which we refer. Within these noun and verb phrases, further syntactic divisions eventually create the various parts of speech. For example, noun phrases often have nouns, articles, and adjectives as parts, and verb phrases are often partitioned into prepositional phrases, verbs, and adverbs. Consider the following example sentences, most of which describe an event:[2]

1. I ate the apple.

2. I am eating the apple.

3. a) The apple tastes tangy.

   b) Apples taste tangy.

   c) Apples are tangy-tasting.

4. *The apple is a fruit.

The first statement is clearly the description of an event: its boundaries are fairly well-defined in both space and time. The second statement also represents an event, but its temporal extent is spread out relative to the first (this is the nature of the present perfect tense in English). The role of time in the third and fourth statements is less clear, despite the presence of a verb phrase.

Statement (3a), since it is about a particular apple (as indicated by the definite article, "the"), refers to one or several tasting events. The similar statement (3b), "apples taste tangy", is not linked to a particular event, and can be viewed in one of several ways. Viewed as a descriptive statement about apples (or an *extensional* statement), it means that if something is an apple thing, then it is tangy thing. Viewed as an *intensional* statement about the abstract concept "apple", it says that this concept is a part of a larger concept: "tangy".

Statement (3b) might also be understood as statement (3c), where the verb *to be* has been explicitly introduced. In this rendition, the statement seems more likely to be a definitional statement;

as such, it would be a relationship directly between abstract concepts. Finally, statement (4) may also be viewed as definitive of the concept "apple". However, this reading of the sentence is complicated by the use of the definite article, which seems to convey that this particular apple (i.e. whichever apple is indicated) is a fruit, as opposed to conveying the fact that "apples are fruits".

6.2.1: The Sentence

The smallest *valid* reference in the conceptual universe is the sentence.

When we learn the concept "She dances beautifully", do we first conceive the noun phrase and then the verb phrase, first the verb phrase and then the noun phrase, or do we learn both together as a unitized event? Do we learn nouns and verbs by dividing sentence-concepts, or do we learn sentences by combining noun and verb concepts? It seems somewhat odd that despite our overwhelming familiarity with language, these questions are difficult to answer.

Most people probably accept without hesitation that without a dancer, there can be no dance. With a bit more hesitation they might conclude that without a dance, there is no dancer. A dancer does, will do, or perhaps has done a dance. Similarly, a dance has or will have a dancer. Just as thinking requires a thinker, a thinker (by definition) requires thinking. In some sense, it seems that the dancer and the dance are a singular thing: an event which can only be described with a complete sentence, as opposed to either a noun phrase or a verb phrase. If we are forced to be terse, we might also use the gerund *dancing* to indicate the presence of both the noun and the verb. "Dancing" may in turn require something else, but let's stop here for the moment.

The combination of nouns and verbs make a reference more complete. Alternatively, the smallest linguistic referent which can be accurately dereferenced is the entire sentence (as opposed to just the noun or verb phrase). Speaking more loosely, "the apple fell from the tree" in some sense *exists more* than "the apple": the entire sentence is more meaningful than its noun phrase. Alternatively, we may say that noun phrases and verb phrases are more dependent than an entire sentence: something which has both a spatial part and a temporal part is more independent. For example, the composite *doing* is an object: the *doer* and *what is done* are constituents of this that do not exist as (complete) objects. These constituents can be *defined*, but they should only be dereferenced in conjunction with a full spatiotemporal specification; they must be combined in order to validly refer to an object of high dimensionality (i.e. an object in the physical universe).[3]

Again, every concept has at least a partial meaning. However, only some of these concepts are valid references to an object (or a percept). Some words may not be validly dereferenced on their own: although they have some meaning, their referents have a dimensionality that is lower than the space in which they exist (they are dimensionally incomplete). In particular, nouns (spatial things) and verbs (temporal things) do not fully characterize an event (which requires both spatial and temporal ordinates), and so nouns and verbs cannot be independently dereferenced in a world that consists only of events (i.e. four-dimensional things).[4] In other words, language carves the world into space and time by collecting the spatial dimensions into the noun phrase and the temporal dimension into the verb phrase, but they exist only in combination.[5]

To say that certain parts of speech are more meaningful than others entails that in some sense they correspond better to reality. If one takes the position that only entire sentences (higher-dimensional events) *really* exist, what are the consequences associated with falsely believing in the reality of nouns?[6]

The implications of one's answer are potentially significant. If we misunderstand the "natural parts" of reality, then we might be less capable of achieving our desires. Let us assume that if we desire something, then our desire is attached to that thing *as we understand it*. If we like sugar, for example, and we attach our desire to sugar, then it will be fairly straightforward (even if it is not always possible) to get some sugar. Similarly, if we like sugar but attach our desire to salt, we will be unhappy, but still in a straightforward way.

On the other hand, instead of desiring the right or wrong things (i.e. things which did or did not make us happy), we might desire the wrong *type* of things. For example, we might desire things which bring happiness in dependence on some indeterminate relationship (i.e. the objects of our attachment and the things which bring us pleasure are somehow intertwined). In this case, we might both end up in an unsatisfactory position, and have some frustration at having done so. To return to the example of sugar, if instead of chasing after sugar we chase after the color red (because we incorrectly associate it with sweetness), then we are in trouble. While we may get lucky by eating red foods in an orchard, outside of the orchard we may suffer upon obtaining bitter red fruits. On the other hand, if our concepts correctly correspond to objects, we can seek out sugar instead of red things, thereby avoiding this problem.

6.2.2: The Noun Phrase

The noun phrase identifies the spatial extent of sentences.

Noun phrases restrict attention to a particular area of space: traditionally, they refer to a person, place, or thing. While they often take relatively simple forms (such as proper nouns that identify a particular individual), they can also restrict spatial attention by picking out instances of a class (such as count nouns) or by applying shapes to some ubiquitous stuff (such as mass nouns). This section explores the ontological priority of concepts corresponding to proper, count, and mass nouns. As a concrete example, we ask which of the following concepts is ontologically prior: a particular apple (a proper noun), the set of apples (a count noun), or apple substance (a mass noun).

This distinction between proper and count nouns is similar to the distinction between tokens and types. The latter distinction is illustrated by an example posed by C.S. Pierce: in the following picture, how many words are there?

The   The

Figure 6.1: The the

Some people say that there is one word, "the". Other people say that there are two words, one beside the other. The difference between these two points of view is exactly the difference between tokens and types. There is one *type* of word in the figure, and there are two *tokens* of that type. In this case, the question becomes: are tokens derived from types, or are types derived from tokens?

The question of which type of noun is ontologically primary is a psychological version of the philosophical debate regarding natural kinds. Historically, the debate about which things are *real* (i.e. natural kinds) has considered primarily candidates from the set of noun phrases: things which do not have a temporal extent. Ultimately, we propose a model where only event-like things (things with a temporal extent, as opposed to purely spatial things) are candidates for being natural kinds (or things that exist in the physical universe as individuals). Here, however, we restrict our attention to the noun phrase.

The First Concepts

The primary notion of identity is called self-identity.

The conceptual hierarchies that we form are rich and pervasive. Initially, however, they are necessarily quite stark: a conceptual foundation must be laid first, and those initial concepts do not appear to be innate. These early concepts are not of inherently greater importance, but presumably they are the first to be learned because they have a high utility to the animal (perhaps they are highly correlated with the perception of pleasure). These concepts may be regarded as simple or primitive, because they are the earliest words in our linguistic evolution, but they are also some of the most influential, in virtue of their role as the edifice of subsequent conceptual structures.

The question of which concepts are learned first is central to the work of the French psychologist Jean Piaget. Piaget studied early human development extensively, which he divided into several different *developmental stages*. The characteristic property of a developmental stage is the ability to form certain concepts (or at least to behave as if one has formed those concepts). Hence, the order of the Piagetian developmental stages informs the study of ontological priority.

The first Piagetian stage is called the *sensorimotor* stage, which occurs during the first two years of life. This stage happens in conjunction with developing basic sensory-motor coordination. One of the important hallmarks of this stage is called *object permanence*: which entails behavior which indicates the understanding that objects *persist*. Objects may move around, and they may go out of our field of perception, but they are understood to still exist: for example, we could find them again, if we went looking for them. In other words, we develop the concept of "an object which exists independently of its percepts".

Piaget observed that symbolic representation typically occurs between eighteen and twenty-four months of age, at the end of the sensorimotor stage. This developmental stage is also characterized by learning the concept of self/other. The self, understood as the body, is approximately that part of the world that can be directly controlled (i.e. by one's mind). The thing which the child cannot control directly comes to be known as the non-self, or other.

The next stage is called the pre-operational stage, during which children become capable of actions on objects. This corresponds to the formation of many of the first concepts. These will be introduced later as first-order concepts.

At approximately four years of age, reasoning begins. Piaget theorized that during this stage, other selves are recognized *as* selves: children overcome solipsism, and recognize others as individuals. In other words, the concept of other comes to be composed of things which are very much like one's self. This is also the stage during which the ability of the child to learn new words begins to increase dramatically: although symbolic representation began prior to four years of age, language acquisition at that earlier stage is relatively primitive. While a number of concepts or symbols are learned at that time, that stage is not characterized by the exponential increase in vocabulary enabled by the definition of symbols using other symbols.[7]

Self/Other

The primary notion of identity is called self-identity.

One of the first concepts to be created is the *self*, which is formed by partitioning the percept of everything, and which simultaneously creates a counterpart, *other*. The self/other distinction is quite possibly the first dichotomy that we create in the conceptual universe. It is not the same as the subjective/objective distinction. For example, visual perception, which is a part of the subjective domain, does not distinguish between oneself and others: both have an equal footing as visual objects. Also, there are parts of oneself that ordinarily cannot be perceived (such as the hair on the back of one's head, which is a part of one's self).

If the self/other distinction is conceptual, then we are responsible for choosing the location of the boundary. As an example of how the location of this boundary is chosen, this section examines hedonists. We define hedonists as people who maximize pleasure for their self. So, in virtue of their self-identification (i.e. how they conceive of their self), they will act to maximize the pleasure that this "self" receives. Turning this definition around, we might also define a person's self as the thing that benefits by that person's actions (or at least as the thing that is *intended* to benefit by those actions).

Clearly, the definition of hedonism used here is different than the regular definition of hedonism, which connotes a person who does not care about anyone else. Although in both cases hedonists care only about their selves, there is flexibility in what constitutes this self (or self-concept). Hence, there is a difference between these two definitions of hedonism when people consider themselves to be other than just their bodies. For example, although hedonists always act in their self-interest, they will end up acting in someone else's interest if they consider that person to be a part of their self-concept.[8]

To begin with, suppose that I believe my self is roughly identical to my material body. When I am happy and loving myself, I might give myself savory foods, or various other physical pleasures. If I care about other people's opinions of myself, this would translate into caring about my physical appearance. The relations that I enter into with other things are understood on a very physical level. If I compete, it may be by running in a race; if I love, it has a physical expression.

Now suppose that I identify closely with my mind; I deeply value the thoughts and ideas that I have, as they *are* me. My body, its physical pleasures and pains, do not matter as much to me. Caring about other people's opinions might express itself as the desire to communicate my ideas, or to demonstrate my intelligence and originality. Personal intelligence and wisdom (or the lack thereof) become my virtue and vice. I might compete by writing a book, in which I have written a fancy, new-fangled sentence such as this one.

On the other hand, suppose that I identified with my family. This might entail identifying with several people, depending on how big my family is. I take as much pleasure in my brother's gold medal, or my dad's financial success, as if these had been my own successes: I don't care if I personally won the race or wrote the book. This attitude is *self-sacrificing*, in that I would forego my own welfare for that of my family or partner, but only from the bodily-identified view of a self.[9]

As the boundaries of self-identification continue to increase, I might identify with my country and enter the political sphere, or identify with all living things and strive to manifest charity and compassion for all creatures. At the limit, I would consider all things to be my self. This is semantically equivalent to not having a self at all, in that the property of "self" no longer applies to a limited thing.

Proper, Mass, and Count Nouns

Different types of nouns are abstracted from events in different ways, in virtue of which they require different quantifiers.

Most sentences act as references to events in the world; to do this, they employ a calculus of references and abstract concepts. These concepts must ultimately be dereferenced, or made concrete, in order for them to be meaningful and understood: quantifiers serve in that capacity.

One distinction between proper and improper nouns is our familiarity with them. Objects corresponding to proper nouns are literally known on a first-name basis: improper nouns are more abstract. Objects corresponding to count nouns are known to be individuals of some sort, but we do not necessarily have individual names for each one. Mass nouns denote stuff whose substance is known, but whose form is not. The relationship between these different types of nouns is shown in the following taxonomy:[10]

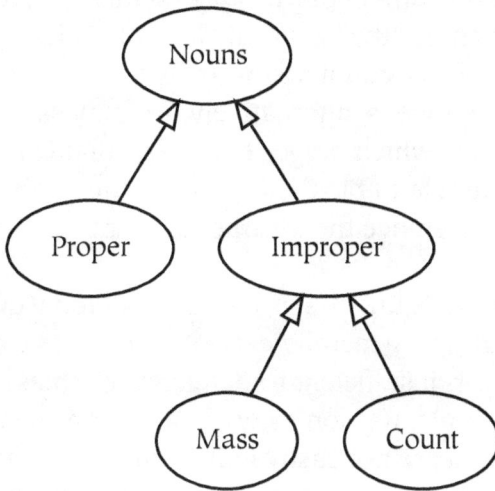

Figure 6.2: A Taxonomy of Several Types of Nouns

Another distinction between proper nouns and improper nouns is related to uniqueness: proper nouns denote *unique* individuals, and improper nouns denotes members of a class (they are unique, the opposite of being generic or abstract). For example, although there are a number of people in the world, there is only one of me. So while I am *a* person, I am also *me*: I have a name which designates exactly myself. Hence, I am simply me: I am not *a* me, *the* me, or a *human-sized portion* of me.

Proper nouns have a name which designates exactly themselves, so they do not need quantifiers. Improper nouns do not reference unique individuals, so quantifiers *are* necessary to do so. In English, this quantification (i.e. the dereferencing of concepts) is often achieved by the use of definite and indefinite articles (the words "a" and "the"). Both articles take an improper noun as an argument, which they dereference or individuate. These articles serve as the inverse of naming operator, in that they are responsible for the semantic transference from a denotation to the thing denoted (or at least one level closer). For example, when one learns the concept of "cat", and one further associates that concept with the symbol "cat", you have named that thing. "Cat" exists as a symbol, and in particular a count noun; to dereference it, an article such as "the" is used; "the cat" is less abstract than "cat". In other words, count nouns are types which are composed of a collection of tokens: alternatively, we may say that there is a dimension of cats, which ranges over particular cats. It is the role of the definite article to pick out a coordinate on that dimension, and thereby dereference the abstract concept.

Mass nouns, as do count nouns, require additional quantification. The indefinite article generally cannot be used as a quantifier for a mass noun: it is insufficient to dereference a mass noun. Using sand as an example, we don't say "*a* sand", presumably because the grains of sand are not easily individuated. On the other hand, the definite article can sometimes be used, presumably because the containing shape is already known if we are referring to a particular volume (e.g. the sand). In general, mass nouns require quantification of their shape or spatial location. For example, "water" is a mass noun whose spatial extent is not discrete: when it is dereferenced, it is typically associated with a particular volume or shape (e.g. "a drop", "a puddle", etc). Although count nouns occur in phrases such as "an apple" or "the apple", mass nouns occur in phrases such as "a drop of water" or "the puddle of water".

The ability to use shapes and substances to refer to things is efficient in comparison to proper nouns, since we can use the adjectives "drop" and "puddle" as containers for any number of liquids: we do not need a different word for each shape-substance pair. "Cow", as an example of count noun, refers to a thing which has a rather characteristic shape. While it is conceivable that cows could have been denoted in English using mass nouns, it seems improbable, since we would end up with some construction like "a cow-shape of cow-stuff". Very little comes in cow shapes besides cows, so there is little advantage in constructing "cows" in this way. If cow stuff comes in shapes other than cow shapes, then it is likely that some misfortune has befallen the cow (note the difference between the nouns "cow" and "beef" in this respect).

Ontological Priority of Nouns

The abstractness of nouns can be quantified by using the notions of dimensionality and conceptual order.

Apple percepts are necessarily ontologically prior to apple concepts, since concepts are formed in dependence on percepts. This assumes, however, that people learn about apples by direct experience with them (as opposed to defining them using other concepts). Between two concepts, establishing ontological priority is not as easy to decide: most concepts are known through a mixture of experience and definition in terms of other concepts. Relatively few concepts (or words) are learned either entirely through experience or entirely through other words. On the other hand, it may be that certain kinds of concepts are *necessarily* ontologically prior to other kinds of concepts. This relationship is of particular interest, as it informs us about the structure of cognition.

This section considers three different kinds of apple concepts and their interrelations. Although apples are count nouns in the English language, we will cast apples as three different parts of speech, each of which corresponds to an apple concept (or a kind of apple understanding). The first kind of concept is the particular "apple", such as "apple$_1$" or "apple$_2$", which corresponds to proper nouns (we use numeric subscripts instead of proper names like Bill or Sue, but they amount to the same thing). The second kind of concept is "apples" (or apple-stuff), understood as a mass noun. It requires some container in order to be understood, as it is a substance without a shape (note that this is not the same as the plural count noun "apples", which has discrete spatial parts). Finally, we have "an apple", understood as a count noun: although we put quotes around both apple and the indefinite article to indicate that it should be treated as a count noun, we are referring to the concept of apple before it has been *counted* (or had the article applied).[11]

Before we examine apple concepts, let us look at several different kinds of apple percepts. The following diagram depicts a partitioned perception of an apple orchard: the percept of 'Orchard' occurs first (at the top), and we perceive individual apples by dividing this larger whole. In essence, this diagram depicts the hypothesis that percepts are composed hierarchically. It is a meronomy, where a given whole is spatially partitioned: this partitioning is informed in large part by vision.

In this example, individual apple percepts are parts of a percept that covers the entire orchard:

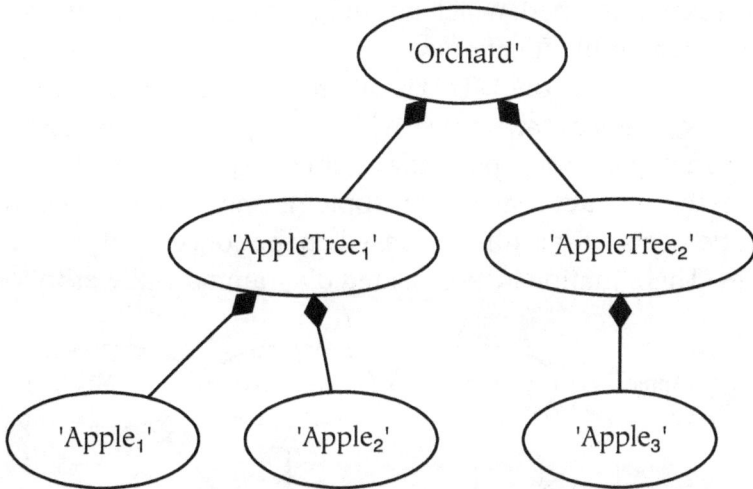

Figure 6.3: Apple Percepts

Consider a number of percepts corresponding to two different apple objects at different times, where each apple is associated with many relatively instantaneous percepts of it. These percepts are denoted with single quotes, and subscripted to indicate that there are many different such percepts. In the diagram above, they are represented as terminal nodes. Our question about the ontological priority of nouns is informed by how these many percepts are collected into the various apple concepts.

Concepts are initially very generic, and they become specific through a process of successive approximation. Studies of conditioning show that at first, the discriminations between relatively similar stimuli are poor. In other words, it is initially difficult to tell apples apart from one another; it is only with increasing amounts of experience that individual apples are distinguished. Conceptually, apples can be distinguished from oranges before they can be distinguished from each other.[12]

This could be taken as evidence that the apple type is learned before apple tokens. In contrast to this, we believe that a concrete apple token is learned, which has many instances: in other words, a perceptual apple function which picks put all particular apples (as opposed to just one). This is different in construction from the abstract concept of "an apple", which is the collection of functions which each pick out a particular apple ("Apple$_1$", "Apple$_2$", ...). Hence, the abstract concept "an apple" is only indirectly based on these percepts, as it is directly based on the concepts of individual apples. This situation is represented diagrammatically as follows:

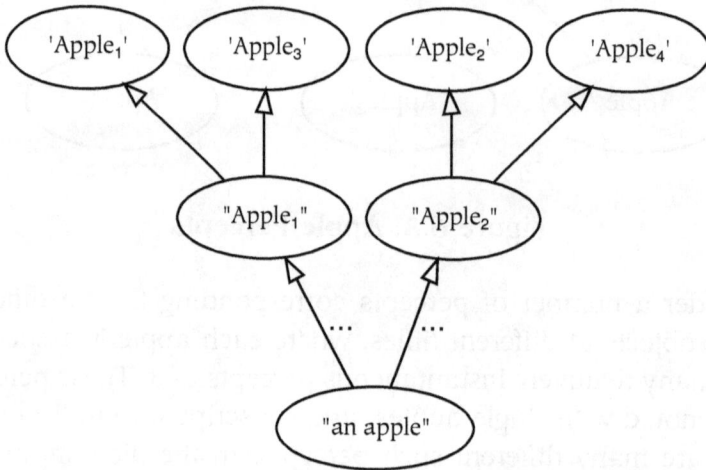

Figure 6.4: Apple Concepts

There are several points of interest in this diagram. The first row represents percepts, where we have assumed that all percepts are of individual apples at different times. The second row represents the concepts corresponding to two particular apples, which are created from a number of percepts (and are functions which operate on perception). A (concrete) concept which did not distinguish between any of these apple percepts would also occupy this level. The third row depicts a more abstract concept, "an apple", which is based on other concepts (the ellipsis indicates that these concepts are not necessarily based directly on these concepts). Ultimately, it is based on the percepts of individual apples, as are "apple$_{1-2}$".

Under this analysis, proper nouns are necessarily ontologically prior to count nouns, as count nouns are constructed by collecting proper nouns. Mass nouns, since they require both articles and a shape to dereference them, are more highly abstract. In other words, since they are syntactically a more refined part of speech, they are almost certain to be learned after count nouns. However, the mass noun "apples" can be based on a percept corresponding to 'all apples': in that case, the mass noun might occupy a lower ontological level.[13]

In any case, the quantification of the informal statement that proper nouns are ontologically prior to count nouns, it is necessary to have some way to formally characterize the difference between them. To do so, the notion of *abstract concepts* can be replaced with the notions of ontological order and conceptual dimensionality (most of the details of this will be left to the conclusion).

Ontological order is directly related to ontological priority: increasingly abstract concepts have a higher order. We will limit the operation which produces increasing ontological order to an operation which collects its contents, such that the dimensionality of the thing increases every time the ontological order of the thing is increased. In other words, every concept which we form based on previous concepts has a dimensionality one higher than the concepts on which it is based. "An apple", as represented above, is a concept which references (and ranges over) individual apples. This abstract concept, because it is based upon concepts of individual apples, requires an increase in the conceptual dimensionality (this may be likened to mathematical integration). Similarly, each individual apple ranges over a set of apple percepts, and is therefore also of a higher dimensionality.

Let us assume that each apple percept is three-dimensional, and that there is a generalized concept corresponding to these percepts (e.g. an individual three-dimensional apple such as "$apple_1$"). When a number of these individual apple concepts are collected, it is possible to form a (more abstract) four-dimensional concept (the fourth dimension is essentially an index over the particular apple concepts). Definite or indefinite articles (as in "an apple" or "the apple") can be used to reduce this dimensionality, so that it once again becomes a three-dimensional thing. In other words, when articles are applied to count nouns (which are abstract), they move us out of the conceptual realm (or at least one order closer to the perceptual realm): they dereference references. For example, articles make count nouns as concrete as proper nouns: they make them less abstract, and thus closer to our perceptual reality.

6.2.3: The Verb Phrase

The verb phrase is the temporal part of sentences about events.

Verb phrases enable sentences to refer to events by describing the movement of the noun phrase through time. Adverbs further restrict the temporal extent (and action) identified by the verb, just as adjectives restrict the spatial extent identified by the noun. Prepositional phrases modify the verb (was beaten *with a stick*), just as adjectival phrases modify the noun (the boy *that threw the rock*). This dynamic creation of concepts allows us to bypass creating symbols that represent each individual concept. In this section, we explore a modification of verbs themselves which allows their dynamic construction: transitivity.

Transitive and Intransitive Verbs

Verb phrases may be intransitive, in which case the verbs are semantically complete, or transitive, in which case the verbs require an object.

Verb phrases take part in two basic kinds of sentences. They can add an action (and a temporal aspect) to the noun phrase and thereby create an event which references the world, as in "I ate", or they can define the relationship between two concepts, as in "an apple is a fruit". This section considers the role of verbs only in the former type of sentences.

If verb phrases were constrained to consist of single verbs and nothing else, they would be quite limited in expressive power. If only one-word verbs existed, then the number of verbs needed to describe the temporal behavior (or action) of the things referenced by nouns would be enormous. Adverbs allow us to decrease the required number of verbs to express a given amount of information substantially (in fact, by an exponential amount). For example, if we have four adverbs, each of which can apply to four verbs, we must learn eight words. However, this allows us to construct sixteen different verb phrases from these eight words (counting only the verb phrases that can be formed with a single adverb).

Verb phrases can also be constructed by using a combination of a noun phrase and a verb phrase, which offers an expressive efficiency similar to that of adjectives. The verbs which require an object (or noun phrase) are known as transitive verbs. These constituent noun phrases play the grammatical role of the object of the sentence, as opposed to the top-level noun phrases, which play the grammatical role of the subject.

Syntactically, transitive sentences have a part structure which is decomposed into two parts: a noun phrase and a verb phrase. Grammatically, these sentences are broken into three parts: a subject, verb, and object. [14]

Under the assumption that syntactically simpler parts of speech are of an ontologically lower level, intransitive verbs are ontologically prior to transitive verbs. Grammatically, transitive verbs and their objects combine to play the conceptual role played by intransitive verbs. Syntactically, this is equivalent to the rule that a verb phrase and a noun phrase can reduce to play the same part of speech as an intransitive verb phrase. As an example, consider the phrase "Isabella loves bunny". The deep structure of this sentence is such that "loving-bunny" is a single conceptual unit which is then combined with Isabella.[15]

Considering transitive verbs to reduce to intransitive verbs is an example of using syntax as a guide to ontological priority: generally, simpler syntactic constructions are ontologically prior to more complex syntactic constructions, where the complexity is determined by the fewest number of production rules required to derive a given part of speech. We must learn simple parts of speech before parts of speech which derive from these earlier parts of speech. Concretely, because intransitive verbs play the same conceptual role as transitive verbs in addition to an object, but the former are syntactically simpler, we have good evidence that intransitive verbs are ontologically prior to to transitive verbs.

Notes

[1]These statements are logically equivalent because they express the same underlying structure. They rely on exactly the same dichotomies, so conclusions about the thing on one side of a decision boundary entail conclusions about the thing on the other side.

[2]The linguistic analysis in this chapter is restricted to the English language.

[3]We use the term meaning somewhat loosely in this context. However, the distinction between incomplete and complete (or at least more complete) meaning can be easily understood by an analogy: although the adjective "quick" has some meaning, it is incomplete. It begs the questions "quick what? What is it that is quick?". For nouns ("me", "you", "the apple"), to be incomplete entails that they would raise similar questions: "I did what? What did you do with the apple?" For most people, nouns are not recognized as being incomplete. This seems to be a mistaken view: nouns are not just incomplete in terms of sentence structure, but in terms of meaning. Noun phrases are not (merely) conceptual aggregates of smaller parts: they are parts of a larger whole.

[4]At least, nouns and verbs cannot be dereferenced in isolation from one another, since proper parts must have a dimensionality equivalent to the thing that contains them.

[5]It may not be correct to attribute the separation of the world into space and time to language. Perhaps our perceptions are capable of relaying only the spatial part of the world to us, so time itself (even though we hold it to be an aspect of everything) must be reintroduced to our awareness through the operation of cognition (i.e. since perception cannot do so). In this case, it is language which reintroduces time to lower-dimensional percepts. The difference between these two views amounts to whether percepts are considered to have a temporal component.

[6]This question is related to the philosophical question of natural kinds. To ask what things are natural kinds amounts to asking, "Which concepts are naturally-existing objects in the world?". To believe that there are natural kinds is to believe that the world can be partitioned into into these and only these objects.

The belief in natural kinds creates at least two positions in philosophy: one which asserts the reality of universals, and one which asserts the reality of particulars. The most well known advocate of the reality of universals was the Greek philosopher Plato. For a Platonist, *universals* (such as appleness) are real, and *particulars* (individual apples) are products of the mind. The opposing camp (particularists) believes that the characteristic of *appleness* is an abstraction which lives only in our conceptual understanding, and that only individual apples are real.

[7]Finally, the third and fourth stages take place (the concrete operational and formal operational stages), which enable higher abstract reasoning; these stages

are understood in the current work as an ability (through the use of syntax) to form thoughts out of parts of speech which have an increasingly high dimensionality.

[8]Most people say that the self is the body or the mind (or both), and that actions for the benefit of others are done out of love. That is a bit difficult for me to understand (I am told that I don't understand because I am a man). In any case, here we assume that everyone acts in self-interest, and that when someone loves something, that thing is considered a part of their self.

[9]To be clear, the "self" in "self-sacrificing" is not the self-concept that encompasses something larger, such as one's family. Self-sacrificing applies to a limited notion of self, which might more suitably be called body-sacrificing or ego-sacrificing.

[10]Mass and count nouns, besides being less familiar, are syntactically more complicated: they require articles. This fact does not necessitate that proper nouns are conceptually prior to improper nouns, but it does lend a certain amount of evidence.

[11]We do not consider count nouns to be strictly equivalent to proper nouns that apply to multiple objects: the concept of "an apple" is not the same as the spatially-discontiguous object *apples*. This distinction is subtle but important: apples is the mereological fusion of all apples, but the concept of "an apple" is abstract and must use an article (such as "the") to refer to a physical object: it represents the set-theoretic sum of all individual apples.

[12]It seems fair to say that most people, at least implicitly, believe that the abstract concept of "apples" is derived from a set of individual "apples". Whether people believe in a set of apple objects in the world, as opposed to an object which consists of all of the apples, is less certain. According to the nominalistic or agnostic view, there are no objects inherent in reality: reality is cut into parts by our concepts. However, there are certain parts which are more useful to denote than others; to act in terms of the objects which we name has pragmatic value.

[13]This sort of speculation is of course risky without more linguistic evidence and formal experimentation. The ontological priority in this example may vary from individual to individual, or from culture to culture. For example, if we grew up in an apple orchard and were exposed to truckloads of apples instead of relatively isolated apples, we might be more prone to learn apples as a mass noun.

[14]Conceptually, is the sentence a two-part thing or a three-part thing? In some sense, it seems reasonable to conclude that the transitive sentences have both two and three parts, depending on the level of analysis. From one point of view, only one concept is held in mind at any one time, and as the sentence corresponds to that single concept, it does not make sense to speak of *any* constituent parts. However, that sentence has a hierarchical structure, and any node in that hierarchy can be viewed as an intermediate concept, which exists during the formation of the final concept (which corresponds to the entire sentence).

[15]Languages such as English dictate a subject-verb-object order where the subject is provided first, the verb is next, and the object (if present) is in the terminal position. The next most common class of languages are those that arrange those

parts of speech as subject-object-verb. Languages which separate the verb and the object are infrequent, which provides linguistic evidence for the fact that the verb and the object constitute a single conceptual unit.

Part III: References

References are relations which are capable of bridging universes.

Between two universes, references may occur in both directions. This part of the book is an analysis of the four relations (listed below) between the universes determined by the physical/subjective and the subjective/conceptual dichotomies.

Perception: $\xrightarrow{\ \Psi\ }$

Communication: $\xrightarrow{\ \Delta\ }$

Conceptualization: $\xrightarrow{\ \Phi\ }$

Naming: $\xrightarrow{\ \varepsilon\ }$

Chapter 7: Subjective/ Objective References

Between the objective domain and the subjective domain are two primary relationships: perception and communication.

For things in the physical universe to be present in a given subjective universe means that those things must correspond to references in the subjective universe of an observer. This process of referencing is called perception. The process whereby references to perception are in turn created in the world is known as communication.

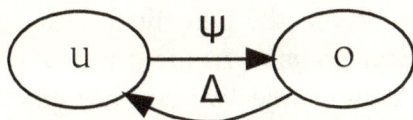

7.1: Perception

Perception is that process by which objects in the objective world are represented by percepts in the subjective world of an individual.

The subjective domain is a point of view in which everything that exists is a reference to something (in addition to being something in and of itself). Your neurons may fire in the objective domain, but in the subjective domain, you have the experience of something (i.e. something referred to by those neurons). Although these descriptions refer to the same event, the language of the description is different: they differ in their point of view (i.e. their point of reference).

Ultimately, the perceiver, the perceived, and perception are all parts of the physical domain. At the physical end of perception are objects, and at the subjective end are percepts. In between these two endpoints, substantial transformation takes place: percepts and objects are very different from one another. This transformation is generally thought to be a passive process, such that phenomena from the world are conveyed relatively directly to an observer. However, there are a number of phenomena which demonstrate that it is also an active process: we influence our perception of the world. In cognitive science, cognitive influence on perception is called *top-down*, and the contribution of the senses is called *bottom-up*.

Bottom-up Perception

Percepts are caused, to some degree, by the objects that they reference.

Percepts of the subjective domain are caused by objects of the physical domain (objects are not the only cause, but they certainly play a causal role). In this way, information from the physical domain is represented in the subjective domain. As the subjective world has a limited capacity to represent all of the features of the objective world that it perceives, percepts represent a limited number of features of the physical world.

Although it is relatively clear that we perceive some small fraction of what there is to perceive, we have a tendency to believe that what we do perceive is relatively undistorted. While what we perceive is more or less consistent from moment to moment, it is not clear what it would mean to be entirely undistorted in this context. There seems to be an uneasy tension between the fact that we perceive electricity in the form of neuronal discharges, and at the same time the world does not appear like a lightning storm. Two of the primary requirements for the relations between the world and our perception of it is that they are consistent and isomorphic. Although our percepts of 'green' may have very little physical resemblance to the wavelength of light in the world, things in the world which are greenish are consistently perceived as greenish.[1]

The isomorphism between percepts and objects can be illustrated by considering a rainbow as it exists in reality and in our perception. The rainbow in reality reflects photons of varying wavelengths: the photons at the frequency which corresponds to 'orange' occur to the right of those photons with a 'yellow' wavelength and to the left of those photons with a 'red' wavelength. Regardless of the medium in which those colors are represented in our experience, this order is preserved: orange is to the left of red and to the right of yellow. This preservation of order is an isomorphic relationship between the structure of our brains and the structure of reality.

Top-down Perception

Percepts are caused, to some degree, by the mind in which they occur.

The role of our minds in both what is perceived and what is not perceived (through attention and inattention), not to mention *how* things are perceived, is often grossly underestimated. The eyes do not act as a mere window, letting information through without distortion. Further, the distortion that is introduced often goes unnoticed. To notice what you do not notice takes rather extraordinary investigation. As an example of how perception can be distorted without being cognizant of it, we will look at blind spots: literally, areas of the visual field that are not perceived.

In order to see one of your blind spots (or perhaps, in order to not see it), look at the following figure. Then, close one eye, and look at the dot on the same side as the closed eye. Then, move the book slowly towards, and then away from, your face. At a distance of approximately one foot, you will notice that the dot that you are not directly looking at has disappeared from your visual field.

Figure 7.1: Blind Spots

These blind spots (there is one in each eye) are created by a small patch of missing retina: therefore, the area of the visual field which is mapped to this patch is not perceived. The optic nerve, which relays optical information to the back of the brain, connects to the retina a bit to the inside of the point directly behind the pupil, on the back of the eye. This creates a literal blind spot (i.e. a spot where there is no retina). Blind spots are odd things, since you do not perceive blind spots. To call them things at all is a bit problematic, since they are characterized by a *lack* of being present. If you pass a pen over the blind spot that you have identified in the experiment above, you will not see a hole in the pen; the missing part of the pen is continued by your mind. A blind spot is a hole that you do not see, and that you have no awareness of. This phenomena is massively exacerbated for people who have suffered certain brain traumas called hemifield neglect. In that disorder, an entire half of the person's body behaves like a blind spot: further, all of perception is affected, not just vision.[2]

The phenomena of blind spots might be characterized as a perceptual deficit, in that there is something wrong with, or missing from, the bottom-up pathways. But the top-down pathways are clearly also implicated in that they cover up the spot with a bit of hallucinated reality. As a result of this top-down influence, reality conforms to our understanding. For example, consider the following question:

What part of your mind are are you using?

The world as we perceive it is not the world as it is; the act of perception is often, if not always, a process to which we contribute. We filter what we perceive, and make it comprehensible to ourselves. Through this process of comprehension, our perception of reality is altered to a nontrivial extent. This alteration is not necessarily a bad thing, but it is unfortunate that we forget that we have altered it. To return to the question preceding this paragraph, we note that most people who read the sentence for the first time believe that it is identical to the following sentence: "What part of your mind are you using?". It is not: the sentence at the top of the page does not make sense, as it is not syntactically well-formed. However, most of us *make it make sense*; we alter it to conform to our expectations and understanding. This alteration is sometimes helpful, precisely because it helps us to understand: extraneous features are eliminated. It is also somewhat detrimental, because it limits our views of reality: it makes us less able to see what we do not understand.

The notion of playing a creative role in what we perceive can be disturbing, although it clearly appears to be true. Dreaming and hallucinations are rather extreme (and interesting) examples of this phenomena: they show that no external cause is necessary for perception. Often, there is no apparent external basis for dreaming about a particular thing at the moment of the dream. The dream of an apple arises without an apple. Of course, this does not contradict the usual case in which the percept of 'apple' arises when a physical apple is present. However, if the percept can occur without the presentation of the object, the causal relationship between these two things becomes less direct (or more tenuous) than we might otherwise have thought. If percepts do not necessarily depend on objects, we are led toward a somewhat unsettling observation: we have no way to tell if we are dreaming or not. This thought led Confucius to make the following famous statement:

> Once I, Chuang Chou, dreamed that I was a butterfly and was happy as a butterfly. I was conscious that I was quite pleased with myself, but I did not know that I was Chou. Suddenly I awoke, and there I was, visibly Chou. I do not know whether it was Chou dreaming that he was a butterfly or the butterfly dreaming that it was Chou.[3]

In dreams, we perceive our environment as clearly as if we were awake. This seems to indicate that perception, even when we are awake, is very indirect; in some sense, we live in a perceptual world, where percepts bear little (intrinsic) resemblance to objects. God only knows what *actual* objects look like: our percepts are to some extent created within the confines of our own heads.[4] Although this realization may initially feel alarming, remember that there is most often a valid, consistent isomorphism between objects and percepts: percepts almost always refer to objects. So even if we are in some sense hallucinating, we can take comfort in the fact that we are more or less hallucinating *correctly*.

The relative contributions from bottom-up and top-down perception are hard to determine. Perhaps our concepts have a relatively small top-down role in perception when compared to the bottom-up role of objects. Even in that case, however, they retain an influential role in guiding attention to what is perceived. Our concepts direct our attention to some things and not others, and therefore we perceive some things and not others. So even if cognition does not strongly influence the *way* we perceive, it still strongly influences *what* we perceive.[5]

Given that reality seems to conform to our understanding, we might ask if this is beneficial: do we *want* reality to conform to our understanding? On one hand, this is beneficial. If we conceive of something as a dangerous snake, even when it is not a snake, this tendency to misconceive things might keep us alive in the event that we see an actual snake. On the other hand, if the world always conformed to our understanding, our understanding would not grow: we would always recognize only those things with which we were already familiar. If we do not perceive anything which we do not already understand, this overuse of the sense-making part of our mind would prevent learning. Although it seems paradoxical, there is a sense in which greater understanding can be achieved by (temporarily) not-understanding.[6]

7.2: Communication

Communication is that process by which events in the subjective world of an individual are represented in the objective world.

The function which maps from the perceptual domain into the objective domain is known as communication. Both symbolic and sub-symbolic information can be communicated to the external world, but this section focuses on the external representation of symbolic information. A language is necessary for symbolic communication, and to the extent that we identify thought with language, language is also necessary for thought.

Communication is complicated in part because the concepts of the speaker and the listener are not identical, even for identical words. It is also complicated if the listener does not know all of the words that the speaker uses. However, the former issue is the more insidious of the two problems, since the listener recognizes the words that the speaker is using, but associates them with different definitions. In light of this, the listener incorrectly believes that he or she understands the speaker's intended meaning.

Speakers of the same language have concepts that can be verified to apply to the same things (at least approximately). It is not clear, however, that their percepts are the same. For example, when you see an apple, and I see the same apple (from the same perspective), do we *see* the same thing? In other words, for identical objects, are our perceptions identical? There is no way to be sure. We might communicate with one another in order to arrive at an answer. Using communication to verify this hypothesis, however, causes at least two problems: the first difficulty is the mapping between the apple object and the 'apple' percept (which occurs internally for each of us), and the second difficulty is the mapping between the 'apple' percept and the "apple" concept (without which we would not be able to communicate our experience of the apple). Both of these problems are captured in the following more generic question: is it possible to ensure that we are having the same subjective experience upon seeing the same apple?

Isomorphism of Individual Perception

Between referential domains, the only available conditions for identity are those of isomorphism.

If you and I have percepts of an apple that are isomorphic to one another, as well as concepts and symbols that are isomorphic to these percepts, then we will not be able to tell from our descriptions if we are having the *same* experience when viewing the same thing. We will both say that we see an apple. If the apple is red, then we will both verbally agree on that point. However, this agreement about the redness of the apple does not help to answer the question; it only transforms the question to "When we see a red thing, does the redness appear the same to both of us?". This train of thought merely transforms the original question into other related questions, in a circular way. Ultimately, all we can be sure of is that the relations between the words of the language that we speak are the same (i.e. that our lexicons are isomorphic). Identity, as opposed to isomorphism, cannot be achieved in this way.

To carry this thought experiment a bit further, suppose that our perceptions of green and red are switched. In other words, what you see when you look at a red thing looks like what I see when I look at a green thing. This does not mean that you are allowed to run lights while driving: "Red means stop" still applies to both of us. Similarly, we both call the same things red: when we learn language, we learn to link a word with our subjective experience of that thing, *whatever that subjective experience may be.*

Now suppose that I could somehow directly perceive your percepts when you look at an apple: would I recognize that object as an apple? Is it possible that it looks, to me, like what I see when I look at an orange? This seems unlikely at first, but we cannot rely on color to distinguish between the two since orange and red might be switched. Similarly, various other properties (in addition to color) might be flip-flopped for us. So how can we be sure? This problem is exacerbated by the fact that we do not need to have a real object present in order to generate the percept in us (e.g. as happens when we dream or hallucinate).[7]

This situation is graphically depicted in the next two figures. In the following figure, we have depicted the objects, the 'percepts', and the "concepts" that correspond to an apple and an orange for a particular individual.

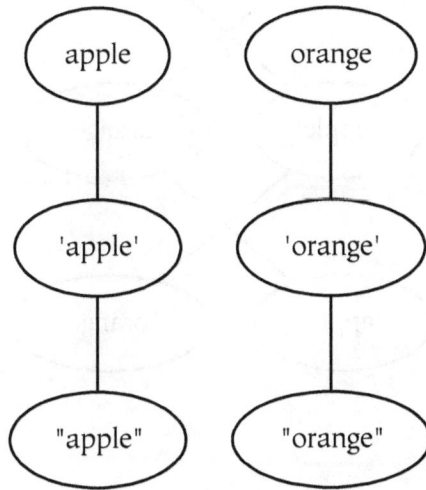

In the following figure, the perceptions of apple and orange are switched. The difficulty in distinguishing between these two diagrams is that, at the conceptual level, there is no observable difference in the mapping from objects to concepts. In both cases, the concepts correctly map to their intended objects. The difficulty is that because we cannot directly perceive the percepts of the individual, we have no way to know the organization of the internal mapping. In other words, the middle layer of perception cannot be seen by an external observer: it is a hidden layer.

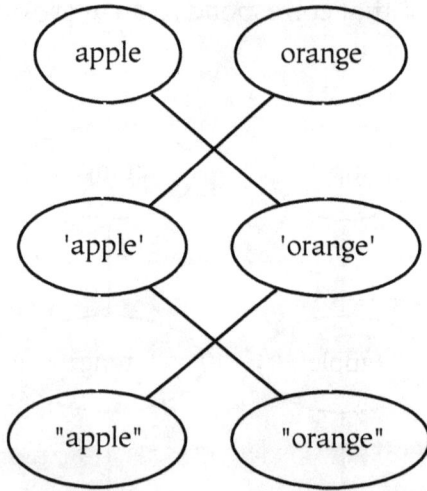

Notes

[1]Brightness, as another example, is a monotonically increasing function in each universe. The study of these mappings between the objective and the subjective, in which various relations are preserved, is known as psychophysics.

[2]Agnosias and aphasias have been popularized by Oliver Sacks in the book *The Man Who Mistook his Wife for a Hat*.

[3]A Source Book in Chinese Philosophy, Translated and Compiled by Wing-Tsit Chan, Princeton University Press, 1963

[4]Of course, to presume looking also presumes the act of perception, so perhaps the notion of *looking like something in reality*, or in a non-subjective sense, is completely meaningless.

[5]If you are not convinced, I highly recommend watching the video about basketball on the following page: http://www.cognitivesettheory.com/links.html

[6]Of course, we presume that people will do something useful with the leftover cognitive resources like put more energy into perception. Withholding rational thought, if it does not entail something else, is probably not any better than going to sleep.

[7]For vision in particular, this is a poor example because we know that spatial mapping is preserved well into the occipital lobe. In general, apples and oranges have a number of topological features which probably tightly constrain their representation in the brain.

Notes

Chapter 8: Perceptual/ Conceptual References

Between the perceptual domain and the conceptual domain are two primary relationships: conception and naming.

References to percepts are called concepts: the process by which these references are created is called conception (or conceptualization). Percepts can be created which in turn represent those concepts; these percepts are called symbols, and the process of creating these symbols is called naming.

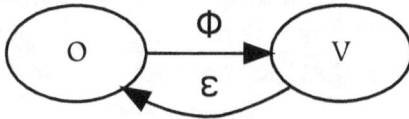

8.1: Conception

Conception is the process of linking concepts to percepts, such that a set of percepts are identified by some concept.

Conception is the process of creating referential associations between concepts and percepts. On the one hand, it may be viewed as the creation of a concept corresponding to some number of pre-existing percepts. On the other hand, it may be argued that concepts are to some extent responsible for creating individual or unified percepts out of the field of perception in the first place. In other words, it may be that the creation of perceptual things (percepts) is due in part to the atomic influence of concepts. This is similar to the nominalistic position, although nominalists make the further claim that the reason independent *objects* appear to exist in the world is that they correspond to individual concepts.

In comparison to percepts, concepts are primarily symbolic as opposed to sub-symbolic: they are categorical (atomic) as opposed to non-categorical (non-atomic). Note that this does not entail that mind *as a whole* is either categorical or not, which is a rather bold statement with a long history in both psychology and philosophy. Relative to one another, the perceptual mind is *not* categorical, and the conceptual mind *is* categorical (the degree to which the conceptual universe is *necessarily* categorical is debatable). In order to gain further insight into the nature of concept formation and categorical learning, this chapter introduces two prominent models of learning: conditioning and neural networks. The former is more of a symbolic paradigm, and the latter is (primarily) subsymbolic.

The Stimulus and the Response

Conditioning is a popular (extrinsic) model of conception.

The conditioning (or stimulus/response) paradigm in the field of psychology, and in particular behaviorism, has produced a tremendous amount of information about how humans and animals learn and behave in the world. In order to remain objective, behaviorism limits itself to be a science of (externally observable) behavior, as opposed to a science of subjective phenomena. In other words, the organism under examination is treated as a black box, the mechanism of which is not explored. [1]

The psychological literature on conditioning (or stimuli and responses) is critically important to our understanding of learning and behavior. Much of this literature is relevant to the more subjective experience of cognition if we make the further assumption that the internal representation of the conditioned stimulus is identical to a concept. Hence, we assume that certain behavioral outputs (responses) are the result of certain perceptual inputs (stimuli), in virtue of the formation of concepts. [2]

Behaviorism categorizes learning by introducing two basic divisions: stimulus/response and conditioned/unconditioned. With respect to the first dichotomy, stimuli are the input to the organism, and responses are the output. With respect to the second dichotomy, conditioned inputs and outputs are those that have been trained, and unconditioned inputs and outputs are untrained (or innate). These two divisions are combined to produce the following four classes of things:

· The Unconditioned Stimulus

· The Unconditioned Response

· The Conditioned Stimulus

· The Conditioned Response

These four categories began taking shape in some of the earliest studies of conditioning, which were conducted by a Russian scientist named Ivan Pavlov. These experiments studied the relation between hungry dogs, salivation, food, and a bell. [3] Pavlov conducted studies of how stimuli became linked to responses (the observable results of a dog's learning process). Pavlov observed that dogs salivate just before, as well as during, their meal (salivation aides the digestion of food). After striking a dinner bell immediately prior to the presentation of the food (on a number of different occasions), dogs begin to salivate in response to the bell, even if the food is not subsequently presented. At this point, the dinner bell has become a conditioned stimulus, which elicits salivation independently of the unconditioned stimulus. In this way, the dinner bell has become a *sign* of food, and it elicits the same response that was originally elicited by the food itself.

Stimuli become linked to responses in virtue of their significance and desirability to the organism, as well as several other factors. The significance of the feeling or feature affects the rate of learning: if something is not significant, then there is little reason to learn it. For example, rewarding someone with food when they are in a state of hunger causes learning because it induces a change in a biologically-relevant dimension (i.e. being satiated). Punishing someone by removing food also causes learning because it induces a change in a biologically-relevant dimension. In this sense, reward and punishment are opposite ends of a single spectrum.[4]

In addition to the significance of a stimulus (as either a reward or punishment), there are several other factors which determine whether a conditioned stimulus will become associated with an unconditioned stimulus. One of the most important of these factors is the time of presentation: a stimulus will only be learned if it has predictive value. Clearly, for a conditioned stimulus to have predictive value, it must appear *before* the unconditioned stimulus: if it appears at the same time, then it has no predictive value (i.e. there is no information above and beyond the unconditioned stimulus itself). In other words, stimulus-response learning anticipates causality.

The predictive value of a stimulus decreases with time; it is difficult to notice the predictive ability of a conditioned stimulus if that stimulus occurs too long before the unconditioned stimulus. For example, if a dog's dinner bell were to ring exactly a year in advance, it is of little predictive value (unless the dog in question has a rather excellent memory). The frequency of the pairing of the conditioned and unconditioned stimuli is also an important variable: a certain amount of time after the stimulus appears, the response is expected to appear, based on the likelihood of past co-occurrence.[5]

In subjective terms, if hunger in the past has always been preceded by not eating (i.e. the absence of features which indicate eating), and fullness preceded by eating, the *eating* concept is learned, and this concept itself will acquire a positive value (which is transferred from the desirability of eating). This kind of learning depends on recognition of the stimulus: it must be possible (operationally) to tell when it is present, or have a cohesive concept of it. As experience with the stimulus increases, the stimulus is more precisely identified; irrelevant or coincidental features of the set are eliminated. For example, if a bell of a certain pitch is the stimulus, but bells with other pitches also ring, the concept "bell" is discriminated from other bells, and thereby becomes more narrowly defined.

Neural Networks

Neural networks are a popular (intrinsic) model of conception.

The conditioning paradigm described in the previous section is incomplete as a general cognitive model for at least two reasons. One is the claim that behaviorism, as formulated, is insufficient to account for the richness of language and verbal behavior. Another is the fact that behaviorism does not describe the biological mechanisms of conditioning (which it avoids on purpose by considering the organism to be a black box). In this section, we summarize a few details from the neural network paradigm, which offers a complementary point of view from which to understand concepts.

The basic principle behind a neural network is quite simple: take a small computing element (a neuron), define its operation, and replicate that neuron in an organized fashion a large number of times, thereby mimicking the structure of a brain. The operation of networks built in this way is often astounding: the exhibited behavior is difficult to predict based on knowledge knowledge of the responsible mechanism. Of course, the mechanism itself is not exactly transparent if the model consists of large numbers of massively interconnected neurons.

The earliest model of the neuronal processing element, the *Perceptron*, is roughly equivalent to a propositional function. This neuron operates on some number of inputs (a quantified input space), and yields a single bit of information, either true or false, as a result. In doing so, the Perceptron creates a dichotomy in the input space: every point in the input space maps to either true or false (later neuronal models typically have a larger range of output values). This output value can in turn be processed by other neurons. This organization, where multiple neurons are neighbors that operate on input at the same time, leads naturally to a *layered* network implementation: neurons in one layer send their output to a subsequent layer, where it is used as input.[6]

A powerful geometric analogy for the operation of these simple, binary-output neurons is that of *separating hyperplanes*. A hyperplane is a division in a hyperspace, or a high-dimensional space (the prefix *hyper*, in this context, indicates the multidimensionality of the thing to which it is applied). In order for the separation (or boundary) created by these neurons to be meaningful, some of the inputs must be on one side of the neuron's decision boundary, and some must be on the other side. The location of this decision boundary is altered by the process of learning, which amounts to a binary classification problem.

In the following picture, a decision boundary is shown with a dotted line. The line approximately separates observations marked 'x' from observations marked 'o':

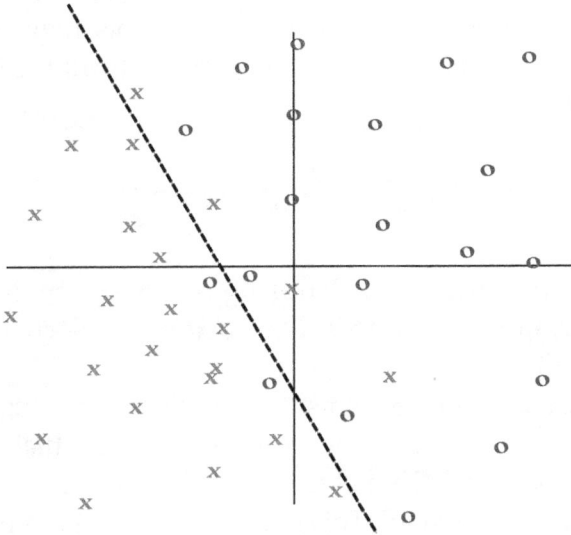

Figure 8.1: A Decision Boundary

The ability to classify individual points (or observations) in the diagram above is equivalent to being able to discriminate the conditioned stimulus: some percepts correspond to the stimulus object, and some do not. To use the Pavlovian example, this boundary might represent a discrimination in auditory feature space between bell and non-bell sounds.[7] In order for this discrimination to be meaningful, we need more than the experience of the bell; we also need the experience of non-bell (otherwise the dividing line would not actually do any dividing). In other words, if everything in the world was a bell, then a bell could not be effective as a stimulus.

Early models of neurons such as the Perceptron are often biologically inaccurate in light of current knowledge. One of the most obvious inaccuracies is the mapping of single neurons to single concepts. Current research indicates that concepts have a distributed representation in the brain. In other words, there is no single neuron that corresponds to the concept "apple": rather, the concept "apple" has a distributed representation across a large number of neurons. So, even though concepts may be atomic from a conceptual point of view, they have distributed physical representations.

8.2: Naming

Naming is the process of denoting a concept by a percept: the percept, in virtue of this denotation, is called a symbol.

Symbols are names for concepts. The process of creating concepts requires percepts for them to reference, from which they are created or abstracted. That concept can be given a name, which is the creation of a symbol. This name (or symbol) is a perceptual representation of the concept: it is in turn capable of further linguistic manipulations. Again, just as a concept becomes a reference for a collection of percepts, that concept can in turn be referenced by a percept: that percept is a *name* for the concept. The recurrent references which are thus enabled by the introduction of naming, when unfolded, become hierarchies of reference. In this way, it is possible to construct concepts based on previously learned concepts, as opposed to constructing concepts based on objects (although in both cases concepts are immediately based on percepts).

The operation of naming is used to define a thing. However, it does not always *introduce* that name; a thing which already has a name can, by being associated with some additional concept, be redefined or have its definition augmented. So, although this operation is one of naming, it should also be viewed as an operation of definition (or redefinition).

Animal Cognition

Animal cognition is a part of human cognition.

Talking about the experience of animal cognition is inherently difficult for at least two reasons. First, animals are reticent to talk, so it is not possible to hear about their experience. Second, although humans do talk about experience, they are not *merely* animals, so it is difficult to isolate the experience of animal cognition from other human characteristics. From a subjective point of view, it is difficult to say which aspects of our cognition are crucially human and which are not. Hence, some amount of speculation is therefore necessary.

What might explain the difference between animal and human cognition, especially when the neuroanatomical differences between these closely related species often do not appear significantly different? Functionally, one relatively uncontroversial and essential difference between animals and humans is the human capacity to learn words. This distinction, which we identify with the operation of naming, is regarded here as a predominantly human characteristic that is responsible for symbolic thought.

The operation of naming is related to the distinction between signs and symbols. Non-human animals are capable of emitting or responding to dozens of words or phrases (e.g. 'sit', 'stay', 'play dead', etc), but their understanding of these words may differ significantly. In particular, most animals understand words as signs, as opposed to symbols. Symbols *are* or *stand for* something: symbols ultimately stand for sets of experience. In opposition to symbols, signs indicate that something else is impending; they are always embedded in a causal context. As an example of a symbol, the written word "apple" may be chosen to stand for the concept "apple", which in turn is created from percepts of apple objects. The word is a terrifically condensed representation: a short series of phonemes, sufficient to distinguish it from other words, which represents an immense collection of experience. To say that animals cannot form symbols in this sense amounts to the claim that the use of perception for the purposes of representing conception is *the* essential advance of human cognition.[8]

Animals have both percepts and concepts. In terms of percepts, animals may perceive (at least in the bottom-up sense) in a manner almost identical to humans. In terms of concepts, however, the ability of animals is restricted: animals lack the ability to represent concepts with percepts. Hence, they can only form or understand concepts which are directly based on percepts, as opposed to concepts which (indirectly, via percepts) reference other concepts. This distinction between first-order and higher-order concepts is explored further in the next chapter.

As a concrete example of the difference between first and higher order concepts, "Bill hit tree" is a statement about the (temporal) world, while "Bill is human" is a statement about language (or perhaps, the atemporal world). The first type of sentence can be directly abstracted from events. In other words, there may be any number of concrete events in which Bill is hitting a tree, and the sentence may be seen as a generalization of those events. In the second case, though, we are dealing with an abstraction, "human", and further saying that Bill has this characteristic (or that Bill is included in the set of humans). This sentence is *not* an abstraction based on a number of percepts in which we observe that Bill is human (or at least, the meaning of the sentence must change dramatically if we do interpret the sentence in this way). As a result, the cognitive lives of animals are more closely tied to their perceptual lives as opposed to humans.

The conceptual difference between animals and humans may also be quantified in terms of the abstractness (or dimensionality) of the concepts which are able to be formed. Specifically, the conceptual mind of non-human primates cannot understand concepts of a sufficiently high dimensionality to be able to speak most human languages.[9] While animals may generate and understand certain sentences, the syntax of this language is significantly different because the concepts which they can form are of a more limited dimensionality.[10]

One interesting speculation about animal cognition is that it cannot comprehend the notion of time. In other words, perhaps the concept of time is the result of the distinctive features of human cognition: perhaps the high-dimensional concept of time is the result of an abstraction over lower-dimensional concepts. This does not entail that time does not exist in the physical universe, but it does mean that it may not be able to be *directly* abstracted from our perceptions (and hence, cannot be present in the cognition of animals). So although certain concepts are abstract things that do not correlate well with our (relatively more concrete) percepts, they may correlate better to the way objects exist in the world.

The Modality of Naming

Thinking can occur in any modality.

How does naming, the representation of experience in symbolic form, occur? In what modality does it occur?

First of all, let us define a name as a symbol or percept which indirectly designates an object. Using this definition, *names* may occur in any modality: for example, an object may be named by a printed word (or picture, or ideogram) or an audible word. The use of one modality for a name as opposed to another is potentially an individual choice: there are probably people who are biased toward visual thinking (thinking in pictures) as opposed to auditory thinking (thinking in sounds): members of the first group are prone to think *visually*, while members of the latter group think *sonically*.

It seems likely that most people *think in words*: pictures tend to be more perceptual than conceptual. As evidence for this, consider the fact that thought is initially accompanied by vocalization, and subsequently accompanied by subvocalization. This process of increasingly less explicit vocalization evolves to the point at which the actual production of sound and mouth movement ceases, even though thought continues.[11] However, if symbols are truly arbitrary in modality as well as form, there is no reason why symbolic representation could not occur in any modality. One requirement for representation is that, in whatever form it occurs, it can be selectively elicited by that which it represents. Of course, that representation must also be able to elicit what it represents: if we could not retrieve the meaning of a symbol, that symbol could not be used for communication.

Thinking in pictures is indicated by the term visualization: this type of thought is sub-symbolic (as opposed to rational thought). Visualization is not irrational, but neither does it (inherently) possess a subject and an object (as would a word-based form of thought). Although thinking in printed words (i.e. typeface) would possess this quality, it is not clear that anyone does this (although perhaps this is related to the phenomenon of speed-reading).

Finally, thinking of some sort takes place within the body. Perhaps this is so different from rational thought that it does not merit the word "thought". However, the neurons of the body store information just as those of the brain. The body has a nervous system which can operate to some degree independently of the brain (i.e. the enteric nervous system). It adopts postures and defense mechanisms which tend to be both precognitive (i.e. formed early in our development) and which often remain below the level of our awareness. For example, are you aware of your posture right now? If you shift it, does it have some effect on your mental state? Although it may be a stretch to say that the body has concepts, the body is certainly capable of resonating with certain conceptual attitudes. Regardless of where thought itself takes place, the effect of thinking certainly has an influence on the body, just as the body has an influence on thought.

Notes

[1]Historically, examination of internal states could not be done objectively as it could only come from subjective report: behavior, on the other hand, can be directly observed and verified by multiple observers. In an age when we are able to directly observe much of what is going on inside a subject's head with various machines, this restriction of the field of study is less warranted.

[2]Talking of concepts violates the behavioral dictum of treating organisms like black boxes. On the other hand, limiting the examination of subjective experience to concepts does not venture arbitrarily far into the territory of subjective report. Further, from a nominalist point of view, behaviorism is already a subjective science in that the CS is a single object only in virtue of being unified in the mind of an observer. In any case, the formalism presented here is an attempt to open the Pandora's box of subjectivity without unleashing complete pandemonium.

[3]In these studies, salivation is the unconditioned response to the unconditioned stimulus (eating food). The bell acts as the conditioned stimulus; by ringing it just before food is served, it comes to elicit salivation (the conditioned response).

[4]Punishment and reward occupy a single dimension from a cognitive perspective. From a physiological perspective, they may be mediated by different mechanisms (neurons, neurotransmitters, etc.).

[5]The strength of the connection is determined by this likelihood, or the correlation of the conditioned stimulus with the unconditioned stimulus. In fact, there is a significant difference here between the correlation of the conditioned stimulus and the unconditioned stimulus, and the informative value of the conditioned stimulus. In particular, the presentation of the conditioned stimulus, if it is not followed by the unconditioned stimulus, will weaken the association between these two stimuli. However, the presentation of the unconditioned stimulus, when it is not associated with a prior presentation of the conditioned stimulus, will not weaken the association.

[6]Incidentally, this division of neurons into layers appears to mimic the organization of the visual cortex. The visual cortex consists of layers at the back of the brain stacked like five or so pancakes; neurons in one layer receive input from previous layers and project their output to subsequent layers.

[7]The type of discrimination that we have shown above is very simple: it is a line. It generalizes easily to multiple dimensions: in three dimensions, it is a separating plane, and more generally, it is known as a separating hyperplane. There are numerous other types of basis functions: in two dimensions, sigmoids (or s-shaped curves) and radial basis functions (which select circular groups) are commonly used.

[8]It is a dramatic change because it enables the ability to form concepts recursively. By allowing language itself to define new linguistic terms, linguistic structures of arbitrary depth can be created.

[9]Noun phrases tend to be three dimensional (spatial), and verb phrases one-dimensional (temporal). Although abstract nouns and other phrases may require higher dimensionality, these higher-dimensional references are lowered through the use of articles and other quantifiers.

[10]It may be possible to construct low-dimensional languages which animals are capable of speaking, although it is not clear that these would be what we usually think of as languages. For example, such a language might consist of only noun phrases connected sequentially.

[11]Interestingly, the usage of the auditory complex remains necessary for thought: neurological evidence links thought with the language areas of the brain (Wernicke's and Broca's areas).

Chapter 9: Conceptual/ Conceptual References

Concepts can be formed recursively.

The conceptual universe is unique in that concepts can reference concepts. In particular, a given concept can reference *other* concepts: concepts (as with anything else) cannot reference themselves. Further, this process must be mediated by symbols, through which concepts are represented in the perceptual universe.

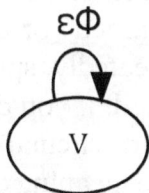

εΦ

V

9.1: First-Order Concepts

First-order concepts refer to percepts that refer to objects; from this reference they derive their semantic value.

There are two types of sentences: sentences about the world and sentences about language. Unfortunately, these types of sentence are sometimes confused with one another.[1]

To understand the need for two types of sentences, let us examine when concepts can and cannot be defined in terms of other concepts. Suppose you pick up a dictionary in order to find the definition of a certain word. It is certainly possible that the definition of the word itself contains a word that you do not know. If you are insufficiently learned (or quite unlucky), you might encounter this problem repeatedly, spending hours trying to find the definition of a single word. If you did not know the definition of *any* words to begin with, the circularity would be complete; you necessarily cannot learn the meaning of any word.

To illustrate the way this vicious cycle is broken, imagine trying to define an "apple" to a child:

Us: "An apple is a fruit."

Child: "What is a fruit?"

Us: "A fruit is a sweet red thing."

Child: "What is a red thing?"

Us: [Hmm...] "A red thing is a..." [what is a red thing, anyway?] "A red thing is a thing that is not blue, green, or yellow."

Child: "What is not blue, green, or yellow?"

Us: [pointing] *"That thing* is an apple. Look. Here."

If we cannot convey the information necessary to define a word using other words, we must point to an actual red thing. In other words, if we are unable to describe a concept with concepts that the child already comprehends, we encourage the child to create a concept based directly on percepts. We could say "Look, that is a red thing", pointing to a red shirt, "that is a red thing", pointing to a stop sign: in this way, the child learns what a red thing is. The child forms a set of experiences in which two things repeatedly co-occur: the percept of a red thing, and someone saying "red thing".

To learn what "apple" is, as a first-order concept, we must have direct experience of an apple and some motivation to learn. If this happens a number of times, we generalize from the set of experiences in which the apple appears. If we enjoy the experience of eating an apple, we might learn that "apple" is a good thing: the concept "apple" comes to be associated with the pleasant eating experience. Perhaps we will learn to speak the word "apple", particularly if that behavior is rewarded: in order to do so, it is not necessary to equate the word with the object.

At some point, however, the word "apple" may become more than just a behavior that is performed in order to get apples. This first-order concept may be named: the utterance "apple" may become a *symbol*, which is capable of evoking the concept of an apple (instead of eliciting a subsequent behavior). This process of using percepts to represent concepts gives rise to a new possibility: language, the calculus of symbols. By performing basic manipulations on concepts using their symbolic representations, we enable the expression of novel concepts (as well as facilitating their formation). These concepts may in turn be given new names, recursively.

To illustrate how sentences are of exclusively two kinds, those that define words and those about events, here are several examples of sentences about events:

1. The apples fell to the ground.

2. Leibniz tossed an apple in the direction of Sir Isaac.

3. You should eat an apple a day.

The first two sentences clearly correspond to events in the world. The correspondence of the third sentence to an event in the world is less obvious. However, given that possibility is a dimension of linguistic reality (at the very least), we may interpret this sentence as a recommendation of a particular five-dimensional event (which may be construed as a six-dimensional event, where the additional dimension indicates some valuation or goodness).

Some types of sentences, such as questions, are difficult to categorize as either events or definitions. On one hand, a question may be viewed as the definition of a word which is intended to be supplied by the answerer. On the other, questions may be understood as sentences about high-dimensional events which vary along a *modal* dimension that spans all possibilities (for more information, see the section called "Constructing Dimensions"). In either case, questions have a part of their specification missing (that part is supplied by the answer to the question). This missing part of speech is indicated with a placeholder such as "what" or "where". The interrogative nature of questions requires the answer to specify a position on that undetermined dimension. For example, "Is it going to rain tomorrow" requires selecting either the true or false coordinate on the dimension of possibility.[2]

To summarize, first-order concepts are categories of percepts. For example, "water" is a concept that we may have learned through the perception (or sensation) of water. While we may later learn the definition of water in terms of other concepts, it is also possible to learn this concept directly (i.e. based on percepts).

9.2: Higher-Order Concepts

Higher-order concepts refer to percepts-that-refer-to-concepts (i.e. symbols).

Ultimately, the meaning of concepts derives from percepts, and the meaning of percepts derives from objects. However, higher-order concepts may be constructed out of lower-order concepts: this construction is made possible by a symbolic calculus which involves both concepts and percepts. For example, while the concept of ice may be known directly to residents of Alaska, it may be impossible to know directly for residents of a hot country without refrigeration. However, residents of that hot country may still know what ice is, by its definition: solid, cold water. Although those residents do not have associated perceptual data (i.e. no direct experience with the referent of the concept), the concept can still be understood. A calculation of references, independent of the things referenced, can produce a result that can itself be both grasped intellectually and subsequently visualized.

This dichotomy between first and higher-order concepts is present in both language and thought, and has been known in many different contexts with different terminology: synchronic/diachronic, knowledge/news, a priori/a posteriori, synthetic/analytic, de re/de dicto, necessary/contingent, etc. Distinguishing between these two types of sentences is vital: to mistake one type of sentence for the other type leads to no end of confusion. For example, if one person were to say "criminals are bad", another person might get upset. But how should we understand this sentence? Is it a statement about the word (or concept) "criminals", and does it define that word? Or is it a statement about a certain kind of person (or object), and does it say something further about their moral (or immoral) character?

Sentences about concepts often take the following form: *word* is a *definition* (or *subset* is-a *superset*). Although the copula *"is a"* is very common in this context, several forms of the verb *"to be"*, the verb *"means,"* and various other words can also be used. Some examples of this kind of sentence are shown below. When reading these sentences, you should interpret them as being definitional (i.e. about concepts), as opposed to contingent statements about the world.

1. Apples are fruits.

2. An apple is a fruit.

3. Apples are red.

4. An apple is a red thing.

In all cases, an object is defined by being a member of a certain class or by possessing a certain characteristic property. In sentences one and three, the phrase *"is a"* is not used, although the sentences can be transformed into sentences which do use the *"is a"* formulation: this results in sentences two and four, respectively. One way of viewing these transformations is simply as a transformation from plural to singular, although in the singular formulation there is the implication that these sentences could apply to any apple.

Statements two and four may be understood as conditional statements about individuals, e.g. "for every thing x, if x is an apple then x is a fruit". In this case, the underlying conceptual structure is potentially quite different: instead of being a relation between concepts, it becomes a relation between objects. This process is called *existential quantification*: it turns relationships between concepts into relationships between objects. It is significant here because it demonstrates how logic reduces sentences about language to sentences about the world. From a cognitive point of view, however, this reduction is not necessary: in fact, in order to accurately model cognition, its universal application is incorrect. There are statements which are purely about language, as opposed to quantified things.[3]

Paradox

Concepts of concepts create the potential for both great understanding and great confusion.

It is paradoxical for something to contain another thing, which in turn contains the original something. However, things can contain references, and those references can refer to things which contain their container. As a simple example, the world contains my head, and I imagine the world. Although it is not the case that both *physically* contain each other, there are valid points of view in which each contain the other.

The ability to defer the definition of references is one of the more powerful features of references, but it can lead to their misuse. Paradox is a fairly direct result of this misuse. The following phrase is a popular example of this misuse, which is known as the Liar's Paradox:

> I am lying.

It seems rather innocuous at first, but it presents a tough question to answer: if we assume it is true, it becomes false; at which point, upon being negated, it becomes true once again. Clearly something has gone wrong here. Why is it that an attempt to answer this question is impossible, or at least leads to an infinite regress?

Probably the most striking thing about this sentence is that it is self-referential: it describes itself. Hence, a reasonable first step in the elimination of paradox eliminates self-reference. Unfortunately, the recognition of self-reference is confounded by the fact that it does not have to be *immediate*; it can be a multi-step, circular phenomena, as illustrated by the two statements below:

1. The statement below is false.

2. The statement above is true.

The paradox in this case is more difficult to spot. The first statement is neither true nor false until we evaluate it. Under the assumption that it is true, we negate the truth of the second statement. This negated statement makes the assertion that the first statement is false, which contradicts our original assumption, and so on: the truth conditions do not converge.

The syntax of a given language dictates how to form concepts. Hence, if a sentence is syntactically well-formed, there is good reason to believe that we can form the concept that it was designed to communicate. However, even for sentences which are syntactically well-formed, a well formed concept is not guaranteed: consider Noam Chomsky's famous example, "Colorless green ideas sleep furiously". Syntactically, we ought to be able to make sense of this; semantically, it turns out to be difficult, if not impossible. This sentence promises the formation of a concept which turns out to be meaningless at best: syntactically well formed sentences may still be semantically vacuous.

Sometimes this conceptual impossibility only becomes clear when we have unsuccessfully tried to form the concept. The paradox of the liar is subtle when it is first encountered; it seems consistent until we try to dereference its symbolic form. Unfortunately, this paradox is one of the easier forms of circularity to spot. For example, suppose you are learning the definition of a novel word, "nifity". If we are told that "nifity" means "not infity", we might conclude that we know what "nifity" means. However, if we have previously learned that "infity" means "not nifity", we may not know what "nifity" means after all. In this case, although there is no paradox, the words are devoid of meaning.

Notes

[1]A sentence may be about objects, percepts or concepts. However, although sentences can be about perception, this seems to be relatively infrequent: if someone tells you about what they are seeing, they are most often making statements about objects themselves (i.e. in the world). Even percepts such as anger are most often directed toward external objects as opposed to indicating our internal states. In this section, sentences about percepts are treated as a special case of sentences about the world, as opposed to sentences about language.

[2]Many questions make use of linguistic variables, which may be understood as references which have not been dereferenced yet: that final dereference is achieved by the answer to the question. So, in the question "who was that in the coffee shop", we may treat "who" as a reference for which a dereference (i.e. a more exact reference, such as a proper name) is sought.

[3]Note that the formulation *is-a*, due to the use of the indefinite article, expresses a subset relationship. By learning those categories of which a word is a subset, we come to understand the word. It may be significant that there is no convenient way to express the superset relationship. For example, the concept "An apple is a fruit" has a fairly easy rendition compared to "Fruits consist of apples and other things". In combination with the fact that the linguistic variable (the word to be defined) occurs on the left, this might be taken as evidence of a holistic point of view (i.e. one which does not build concepts up from smaller things, but rather by dividing larger things). On the other hand, we might simply be observing a tendency to put the (to be determined) linguistic variable on the left hand side in conjunction with an Subject-Verb-Object language (i.e. one which structures its subjects, verbs, and objects from left to right).

Part IV: Conclusion

All things with a beginning must have an ending.

The last part of this book is a synopsis. The first chapter is a brief summary of the important concepts, and the second is a more formal analysis of cognitive set theory.

Chapter 10: Informal Summary

Climb to the top of the tree; enjoy the view.

In this chapter, we present an informal overview of many of the topics discussed so far, and focus on the development of a single individual. To begin at the beginning: when we were new to the world, and the world was new to us, what did the world look and feel like?

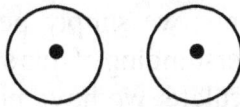

In the beginning, there was only our perceptual universe; in it, we perceive various things, but we do not conceive of them.[1] Conceptually, the world is *undifferentiated*. At this early point in our development, we have undefinable experience. It is a complete experience: there is no alternative to it, and there are no thoughts about it. Talking about it, saying that it is a part or a whole, one or many, is problematic because these words imply a conceptual understanding. Our perceptual mechanisms provide us with various lines, dots, and edges, but we do not conceptually *know* them as such. The world is unique: it just is what it is. Hence, this experience would be inherently hard, if not impossible, to describe conceptually (even if we were intimately familiar with it). We might say that we have not learned to break our experience apart into its constituents; we simply perceive all of it (which avoids an atomistic understanding of this state of affairs). We may also say that it is particulate; we have not learned to unite our experiences into a whole (which avoids a holistic understanding). We might characterize the subjective universe as follows:

Subjective universe: [All experiences and
perceptions within the present moment]

Note that the subjective universe is a referential universe: it reflects (or refers to) various aspects of both self and other in the physical universe (although we do not initially know it as such). The referential mapping from the objective to the subjective preserves something of the metric structure of the world: perception is space-like. In other words, the dimensions of these immediate percepts are space (and possibly time), and all percepts occur within these dimensions.

One of the most significant of the perceptual dichotomies, and perhaps the first, is the self/other dichotomy. At an early age, the distinction is perceptual: we have divided everything into two parts, but we have not understood these two things categorically: there are many percepts of me and many of not-me.[2] We may summarize this dichotomy as follows:

Perceptual universe: 'me'* / 'not-me'*

Despite the fact that in writing this formula we have given a concise label ('me') to a collection of percepts, we do not intend the symbol "me". Hence, it is somewhat unfortunate that we have been forced to use a symbol within these quotes: although it is necessary for communication, it can be misleading. Percepts are spatial creatures, and they are relatively rich phenomena, unlike concepts (it may have been better to represent this distinction with pictures instead of words).

Concepts are formed for classes of percepts which are significant to the animal. In other words, there is a conceptual universe which becomes divided into two mutually exclusive elements, one of which corresponds to the self-concept, and another which corresponds to everything else. As the conceptual universe refers to the perceptual universe, the conceptual distinction between "me"/"not-me" corresponds to the previous distinction between percepts. These concepts are representations which refer to the (many) percepts out of which they are formed:

Conceptual universe: "me" / "not-me"

In this process, an isomorphism develops between a concept and some number of percepts. Eventually, a number of percepts and concepts are formed, many of which are related to one another hierarchically. The divisions which occur are partially determined by their biological importance (this includes things that are most relevant to the individual, such as hunger and thirst). As our conceptual lives develop, biological importance can even become associated with things such as the formulation of philosophical concepts (if, for example, you are employed as a philosopher). Eventually, numerous concepts such as "food", "friend", and "enemy" are created out of the undifferentiated perceptual soup, and figure and ground are separated.

The correlation among the objects in the world induces correlation between the concepts in us (and vice-versa). Some of these relationships are emotionally significant, and concepts co-occur with pleasurable or painful experiences. Concepts may come to be good if they make us or our loved ones happy, or bad if they make us or our loved ones sad: in this way, our world is parceled into desirable and undesirable entities. Objects which occur before others in a fairly consistent fashion, and which are relevant to the organism, cause fairly regular chains of behavior to be formed.

Concepts are internal representations of external stimuli that we learn because they are useful predictors of phenomena that we like or do not like. As we learn more and more concepts, it becomes possible to learn stimulus-response chains: the temporal relationships between concepts comes to approximate the temporal relationships between objects in the world. Because of the isomorphic nature of these relationships, the structure of our concepts comes to mirror the structure of objects (although the choice of the objects that we identify is determined by both us and the world).

The essential thing about the mirroring between a concept and an object is that each stands in the same relationship to its respective context (i.e. its context of concepts or objects): the difference in *form* between concepts and objects is not significant. The isomorphic structure of things persists through several levels of reference. Symbols reference concepts, which reference percepts, which reference objects. The parts at each level influence one another: for example, although objects to some extent determine which concepts are formed, concepts to some extent determine which objects are perceived. Even to speak of objects as independent of a conceptual understanding may give the wrong impression: if the world is continuous and can be divided in arbitrary ways, then to think of the world as decomposable into (only) one object hierarchy as opposed to another is inherently flawed. The fact that we are prone to do so only indicates that our concepts are less permissive of arbitrary division than the world.

The act of perception (or attention) is one of dichotomization. Within the space of that perception, perceptual parts can be produced, which have the same dimensionality. The act of conceptualization is one of unitization: a single concept can refer to numerous constituent percepts or concepts. Despite these characterizations, however, the reverse is also true: conceptualization simultaneously divides its conceptual domain in two parts, the concept and its complement, just as perception collects perceptual features into percepts.

Imagine learning the first-order concept "apple". Having experienced visual percepts corresponding to several different apples ('$apple_1$', '$apple_2$', ... '$apple_N$'), it is possible to form the concept "apple". Initially, when the level of conceptual differentiation is relatively crude, the apple may be recognized as an instance of the (more generic) "food" concept, as opposed to an "apple". Eventually, by acquiring a sufficient amount of experience with different food objects, certain of them are categorized as apples. As our experience increases still further, we learn to recognize specific types of apples, or even particular apples.

All animals have these *first-order* concepts, which are references to percepts that in turn refer to objects. For most animals, the conceptual universe encompasses only these first-order concepts: as symbols are not formed, higher-order concepts are not possible. However, this is where the conceptual universe of human beings is just getting started: humans learn words, or symbols, which are labels for these first-order concepts. This process, whereby we learn words and associate them with objects, is called naming:

"'me'" = "me"

The creation of symbols, in virtue of the ability to form percepts from concepts, allows a referential loop. This cycle allows the formation of higher-order concepts (or metaconcepts). For example, a second-order concept is a concept which refers to a symbol (or percept) that refers to a first-order concept (which, again, is a concept which refers to a percept which refers to an object). There is obviously a lot of referencing to keep track of, but this bookkeeping is rarely explicit. [3]

After a sufficient number of first-order concepts are learned using physical references (percepts), second-order concepts can be learned directly from those concepts. It is at this point that a dictionary first becomes useful. For example, if you know the words "apple" and "juice", you can learn the concept of "cider" without having to drink it: the concepts of "apple" and "juice" can be combined (although to do so requires casting them into a perceptual space). This is a form of thought which involves refining concepts with other concepts. In virtue of this thought (or conceptualization), the direct perception of cider is not necessary (which is necessary for the formation of a first-order concept). This abstraction is the basis of imagination, through which it is possible to construct objects which do not have referents in the physical world.

This conceptual manipulation presupposes the ability to *dereference* the symbols which we form, or to activate the concepts which those symbols represent. Although it is possible to treat symbols as merely percepts, such as running in response to hearing the speech utterance 'run', it is also possible to treat percepts *as symbols*, which allows the retrieval of the original concept. In the first situation, which is representative of animal cognition, the word 'run' is a stimulus to which an animal may or may not respond: animals form a concept which references that stimulus, just as we might form a concept of a stick (i.e. an object). They do not *dereference* this percept to retrieve the underlying concept; hence, they do not derive its *meaning*. For humans, the symbol "run" is *understood* (dereferenced): it triggers the activation of a concept, "run" (which does not derive its meaning from the utterance), but rather from the percepts which were used to create its associated concept.

The use of mathematical notions of space to describe perception and cognition is tremendously useful (not to mention somewhat ironic, since mathematical and logical laws themselves spring fairly directly from basic mental principles). Two of the most significant of these notions for our purposes are *space* and *dimensionality*. The dimensionality of percepts is taken as a phenomenological given: percepts occur with a particular dimensionality (e.g. they are often one-dimensional or two-dimensional). As concepts are references to percepts, their dimensionality when dereferenced is equivalent to these percepts. For example, suppose that binocular vision gives rise to three-dimensional percepts. Concepts which aggregate those percepts are therefore four-dimensional.

By forming a collection of concepts, we are effectively adding a dimension which spans them. Language and syntax rely heavily on this process of abstraction, although their use of dimensionality is rarely explicit. Count nouns, for example, require this additional dimensionality; they are constructed as collections of proper nouns, each of which is a lower-order concept. In this sense, discontiguous entities (e.g. "cats") are not nebulous concepts: they are singular, contiguous entities of a high dimensionality.[4] The syntactic role of various parts of speech, and the division of the sentence into a noun phrase and a verb phrase, is directly related to this notion of dimensionality.

As a final and somewhat Platonic note, although ontological development forms concepts which are increasingly abstract (or which have an increasingly high-order), it may be the case that these high-dimensional concepts are a better fit for reality than their lower-dimensional counterparts. In other words, although more concrete concepts correspond better to low-dimensional perceptions, it may be that more abstract (higher-dimensional) concepts correspond better to the objects which they are intended to reference.

Notes

[1]I am unfortunately speculating here, as I am hardly ever without one concept or another, and my memory is not that good.

[2]It may be that perception cannot be divided without the top-down aid of conception. In that case, this process should be considered as more of a simultaneous process.

[3]For simplicity, it is desirable to talk about the *order* of a percept or concept (where percepts of objects are first order, as are the concepts corresponding to these first-order percepts). There is an implicit assumption here that all *objects* are first-order, which is done as a matter of convenience. It may not be valid: some people may believe that objects in the objective world are higher than first-order. This belief might correspond to whether an individual found the world (objectively) meaningless or meaningful.

[4]Although these statements are to some extent equivalent, the former has connotations of imprecision which are unnecessary.

Chapter 11: Formal Summary

Cognitive Set Theory is a formal description of cognition based on three ontological universes of reference.

There are three universes, each of which is complete from within its point of view. From the point of view of a given universe, all other universes can be represented within it. The physical universe is composed of objects, some of which may be viewed as references to other objects. Certain collections of these references, viewed from a subjective point of view, are known as subjective universes. Within a subjective universe, there are references which constitute a conceptual universe (these references are called concepts). All things are parts of at least one of these universes. Depending on one's point of view, each thing may be assigned to a basic ontological level: either physical, perceptual, or conceptual.

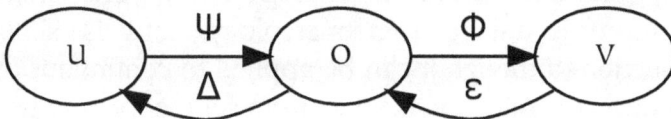

Background

Cognitive set theory is a model of cognition. The formalization of its operating principles relies in large part on mereology, set theory, and linguistics. Cognitive set theory can be grossly characterized as set theory with a mereological understanding of elements: it is a formal model which encompasses syntax and semantics. However, this characterization ignores several important differences:

· Cognitive set theory is cognitive: its primary purpose is to describe cognition, as opposed to establishing a framework for mathematics.

· References (such as concepts and symbols) are introduced in the language explicitly. To do so, the Zermelo hierarchy is reformulated as a two-stage, perceptual and conceptual process.

· Dichotomy and collection are interpreted as functions of perception and conception, respectively. The notion of dichotomy is taken from mereology, and is similar to intersection (although it can be applied to continuous things). The notion of collection is taken from set theory, and is similar to union (although it operates on sets themselves, rather than on their elements).

· There are no axioms related to infinity (infinity is neither affirmed nor denied: it is simply never encountered in practice).

· The restriction to first-order logic is dropped, since it is not appropriate when modeling human languages.

· Syntax and semantics are united under a multidimensional model of cognition, and are formalized in terms of set theory and mereology (respectively).

Set theory and mereology are logics which have complementary strengths and weaknesses. Set boundaries (or curly braces) prevent things like subset transitivity, and make things like intersection somewhat awkward. On the other hand, the tendency of mereology to fuse its parts together is problematic if we wish to keep the parts distinct (which is essential for references): mereology does not have the property of additivity. Cognitive set theory is a proposal for how these two logics can be brought together in a way that mirrors the operation of the mind.

The following sections informally introduce the concepts of universe, parts, and references, followed by a summary of some of the many points of connection with mereology and set theory. This is followed by a number of rules that describe the operation of cognition, which operate in terms of these universes and references. Finally, the relation of this model to logic and linguistics is discussed.

11.1: Universe
U

There exists a thing called a universe, U, which is unique. To differentiate it from other universes, it is sometimes referred to as the physical universe.

The universe is the largest thing, unique unto itself. Precisely because there is nothing else to compare it to, however, it makes little sense to speak of it as *the largest*, or even *unique*. These remedial terms are only appropriate if it is conceived of as *not the largest* or *not unique*. Everything can be divided, which results in parts: it can be divided perceptually or conceptually, regardless of its physical divisibility.

11.2: Reference
$$y = \text{ref}(x)$$
$$x' \equiv \text{ref}(x)$$

References refer to other things (which may themselves be references). The first equation above states that *y* is a reference to *x*. Another way of writing a reference to *x* is to add to it a single tick mark: *x'*. This indicates that the referential level of a reference is one higher than that of the thing to which it refers.

References refer to parts of a universe, as well as being parts of a universe themselves. When they are collected together and understood *as* references, as opposed to being merely things, they have the characteristic property of forming a referential universe. This referential universe is the collection of all references from a particular point of view. As references depend on a particular point of view, there are multiple subjective universes: for example, different animals have subjective universes (or, from their point of view, different animals *are* subjective universes).

Mereology

The set theoretic formalism is particularly good for manipulating discrete quantities, but it is notoriously bad for manipulating continuous quantities. Although it is possible to overcome this deficit with various contrivances, the use of sets in cognitive set theory is restricted to that which they are most suited: discrete things (continuous things will not be discretized in order to apply set theory ubiquitously). The approach used here is to augment set theory, which is used for discrete quantities, with mereology, which is used for continuous quantities.

Mereology is similar to set theory, and was developed at approximately the same time. Although it is not as popular as set theory, it has undergone a good deal of formal scrutiny, and it is regarded to be a solid foundation for formal logic. It is particularly well-suited to spatial logics. Unfortunately, it has historically been viewed as a competitor to set theory, as opposed to a counterpart, so the historical popularity of set theory reduced the potential contribution of mereology.[1]

Mereology literally means the study of parts (*mere* is Latin for part). As opposed to set theory, mereology is characterized as having a transitive parthood relation. For example, if x=pt(y) and y=pt(z), then we may infer that x=pt(z). As previously mentioned, this is not the case for the set-theoretic *element-of* operator (for which transitivity is guaranteed *not* to hold).

Another way of seeing the distinction between sets and parts is to consider the combination of the sets $\{x\}$, $\{y\}$ as opposed to the parts x,y. Suppose that x represents all people, and y represents all animals. The combination (or union) of $\{x\}$ and $\{y\}$ is $\{x\}+\{y\}$: it does not reduce further. The combination (or fusion) of x and y, however, is merely y: since people are animals, adding the part of the world that constitutes humans to the part of the world that constitutes animals does not result in an increase: that part has already been counted. Set braces prevent this combination, because the *set* of people is not a part of the *set* of animals.

11.3: Parts

$$y \ = \ pt(x)$$

$$ref^{-1}(Y) \ \equiv \ pt(ref^{-1}(X))$$

The parts of a universe are known as *things*, and are created from a larger whole using the pt() operator. The pt() operator is not intended to be unique: $pt_i(x)$ is not equivalent to $pt_j(x)$, i.e. all parts are not equal. The first equation above states that there is a relation between two things, y and x, such that y is a part of x. The second equation, which assumes that Y and X are references, states that the thing which is referenced by Y is a part of the thing which is referenced by X.[2]

The notion of parts used here is that of proper parts: a part must be strictly smaller than the thing of which it is a part. The parthood operation is therefore a dichotomizer in that its operation always produces two non-empty parts (a part and its counterpart). This notion of dichotomy leads directly to the definition of negation.

11.4: **Negation**

$$x \equiv \text{pt}(x) \cup \neg\,\text{pt}(x)$$
$$\neg\,\text{pt}(x) \equiv x - \text{pt}(x)$$

Given some parthood operation, pt(), and a divisible thing x, it is possible to separate x into two things: pt(x) and x-pt(x). If x is known, these two concepts may be referred to as simply pt(x) and $\neg$pt(x), as in the first equation above. This may be rewritten as the definition of the negation operator, which is done in the second equation.[3]

Set Theory

Sets are often intuitively defined in terms of collections, elements, classes, etc. Although these may be valid characterizations, the most important point to emphasize from the perspective of cognitive set theory is that sets are concepts. As such, they are things that can be named (by words), and they are also references to percepts (which are in turn references to objects).

Sets themselves are atomic, although they may contain, or correspond to, a plurality of things. This dual behavior is made possible by the fact that they are (single) references to multiple things: they are atomic in the referencing domain, and plural (or at least potentially plural) in the referenced domain. This is indicated by the curly braces that are used to construct sets: these curly braces are ontologically significant, and constitute a boundary which is a discontinuity.[4]

11.5: **Set**

$$Z = \{x, y\}$$
$$Z = \text{ref}(x,y)$$

The first equation above states that Z is the set containing x and y. The second equation states that Z is a reference to x and y. The first equation is understood in a cognitive context as saying that

Z is a concept; as such, it is also a reference to x and y, which we may further assume are percepts. The curly braces which are used for the creation of a set are an alternative notation for the function which creates a reference (which we have called *ref*). The advantage of using the functional form is that its inverse can be denoted relatively easily (which is not the case when using curly braces).

Sets are conventionally defined in one of two ways: either as a formula in a given language (the intensional definition) or in terms of the enumeration of objects which possess that property (the extensional definition). To express this in more psychological terms, concepts can be defined either with perceptual formulas or as collections of other concepts. Ultimately, all conceptual content is referential, and can be traced to perception. Mapping this to the theory of sets, it entails that all extensional definitions of sets in cognitive set theory must involve elements which ultimately have intensional definitions (this is related to the notion of well-foundedness).

11.6: Element

$$x \in Z$$

$$x \equiv \mathrm{pt}_i(\mathrm{ref}^{-1}(Z))$$

The primitive of set theory is the element-of operator, which is denoted $\in$. If a set Z consists of x, then x is an element of Z (this is shown in the first equation above). In contrast to set theory, cognitive set theory does not introduce the element operator as primitive: other operators are used to achieve the same operation. In particular, the effect of the element-of operator can be achieved by selecting a part of a dereferenced set: this is shown in the second equation, above.[5]

11.7: Subset

$$X \subset Y$$

$$\forall z, (z \in X \Rightarrow z \in Y) \wedge (X \neq Y)$$

The element-of operation enables a simple definition of the subset operation. The two formulas above both express the fact that X is a subset of Y: they are similar to the previous mereological formulas in Equation 11.3, "Parts", that express that X is a part of Y. The first equation states that X is a subset of Y, using the subset operator. The second equation defines a subset in terms of its elements, using first order logic: for all entities z, if z is an element of X, then z is an element of Y. It additionally states that X is not equal to Y, which makes X a *proper* subset.

11.8: Atoms

$$\text{Atom}(x) \triangleq \neg \exists z, (z \equiv \text{pt}(x))$$

To say that a thing is atomic is to say that it has no parts.

11.9: Universes

$$\text{Universe}(x) \triangleq \forall y, x \neq \text{pt}(y)$$

The definition of a universe entails that it is not a part of any other thing. It could alternatively be expressed as that thing whose complement is exactly nothing. This has historically been problematic for set theory, because it is easy to imagine things that contain this universe (in mereology, this is not possible). For sets to contain the universe, however, requires that references are formed in another universe (or in more set theoretic terms, the creation of that set happens in another level of the Zermelo hierarchy, where there is a different definition of U).

11.10: The Empty Set (Nothing)

$$\emptyset \equiv \text{ref}(\ )$$

The empty set is a reference whose referent does not exist. A reference which does not refer to anything is known as nothing, or the empty set. Since nothing is unique, it is given a special notation: a zero which has been struck through.

11.11: The Full Set (Everything)

$$\bigcirc^1 \equiv \text{ref}(\mathsf{U})$$

$$\bigcirc^{n+1} \equiv \text{ref}(\bigcirc^n)$$

A reference to the entire universe is known as everything, or a full set. Everything is denoted with an unbroken circle. A set which is a reference to a full set is also a full set, although it is a full set from a different perspective.

Three Universes

There are three universes which merit particular attention from the psychological point of view: the physical universe (U), the subjective universe (O), and the conceptual universe (V).

11.12: Physical Universe

$$\mathsf{U}_{\text{physical}} \triangleq \mathsf{U}$$

$$x = \text{pt}_i(\mathsf{U})$$

There exists a thing called the universe, U, which is unique. It is everything. To differentiate it from other universes which we will introduce shortly, it will sometimes be referred to as the physical universe. Parts of U are called objects.

11.13: Subjective Universe

$$\mathsf{U}_{\text{subjective}} \triangleq \text{ref}(\text{pt}(\mathsf{U}))$$

$$\mathsf{U}_{\text{objective}} \triangleq \mathsf{U} - \text{ref}(\text{pt}(\mathsf{U}))$$

$$O \triangleq \mathsf{U}_{\text{subjective}}$$

$$x = \text{pt}_i(O)$$

A given subjective universe is defined as a reference (or set of references) to the physical universe (a full set). The part that is left over is called the objective universe (this objective universe is clearly relative to that specific subjective universe). Both of these terms may carry subscripts, since there are as many subjective universes as there are individuals.

The subjective universe is denoted with the letter O. The subjective universe is the universe as it is experienced on a subjective (or individual) level. From the subjective point of view, all perception, conception, and even the objective universe are contained in O. By definition, it is impossible for a given individual to perceive of anything outside of O. Parts of O are called percepts.

11.14: Conceptual Universe

$$U_{conceptual} \triangleq \mathrm{ref}(\mathrm{pt}(O))$$

$$U_{perceptual} \triangleq O - \mathrm{ref}(\mathrm{pt}(O))$$

$$V \triangleq U_{conceptual}$$

$$x = \mathrm{pt}_i(V)$$

The third universe is the conceptual universe, which is a part of the subjective universe. It exists in the same relation to the objective universe as the subjective universe exists in relation to the physical universe. The conceptual universe is denoted with the symbol V. Parts of V are called concepts.

Four Referential Relations

This section explores the four referential operations between the universes we have just introduced:

· *Perception* maps from the physical universe into the subjective universe. It creates percepts, which reference objects. It is denoted with the *psy* operator as follows:

$$O \triangleq \Psi(U)$$

· *Communication* maps from the subjective universe into the physical universe. It often entails the creation of symbols in the objective domain. It is denoted with the *delta* operator as follows:

$$u \triangleq \Delta(O)$$

· *Conception* maps from the subjective universe into the conceptual universe. It creates concepts, which reference percepts. It is denoted with the *phi* operator as follows:

$$V \triangleq \Phi(O)$$

· *Naming* maps from the conceptual universe into the perceptual universe: it creates symbols in the perceptual domain, which reference concepts. It is denoted with the *epsilon* operator as follows:[6]

$$O \triangleq \varepsilon(V)$$

In the previous sections, the referential operators were primarily applied to universes to produce successive universes of reference. However useful, this is not the primary role of references: typically, references correspond to *parts* of a larger whole, not the whole in its entirety. Hence, subsequent analysis will be increasingly concerned with the relationships between parts of these universes of reference. Further, because these referential operations take place on known domains, we will often indicate a particular concept as a specialization of the referential operator, as opposed to a specialization of the domain on which it operates. For example, instead of writing $\Phi(o_i)$ to indicate a given concept, we may write it as $\Phi_i(O)$ (and since the domain is known in this case, even more concisely as Φ_i).

11.15: Perception

$$O \equiv \Psi(U)$$
$$x = \Psi_i(\Psi_j(U))$$

The process of creating references to the physical universe is called perception. Perception is denoted by the operator Ψ, it operates on the the physical universe, U, and it informs a subjective universe, O. Perception projects the objective world into the subjective world. It can be thought of as a function which maps the world into a neuronal representation. Typically, it is constrained by attention: we perceive some part of the universe. The narrowing of perception that occurs with attention is modeled as function composition in the second equation above.

In the first equation, perception is represented as an operator which maps from U to the entirety of O (where we intend the subjective universe of exactly one individual). However, this is somewhat incorrect because the entire physical world is not available for an individual to perceive: the domain of perception is some local portion of the physical universe. Although this level of detail is omitted here, functions such as perception are composite operations that can be broken down further. If we assume that attention is responsible for guiding perception, a finer-grained model of perception can be modeled as follows:

$$\Psi(U) = \text{ref}(\ \text{pt}_{\text{attention}}(\ \text{pt}_{\text{local}}(U)\ )\ )$$

For our purposes, the codomain of Ψ is modeled as a single, high-dimensional perceptual space: it has an associated measure, and it is isomorphic to the external world (assuming that our perception is valid). Although perception usually includes modal-specific percepts (such as vision and hearing), here we consider only the perception of these senses as combined in a single perceptual space.

Perceptual space is divided into percepts. Percepts are parts which may be characterized as N-dimensional volumes, the result of dichotomizing a larger perceptual whole. This perceptual dichotomization is nominal, in the sense that it does not result in changes to the physical world when it is applied; it is not intrusive on the thing which is dichotomized. In other words, the division exists in the referring domain only: the "dividing line" itself is not a part of either a thing or its complement.[7]

11.16: Dichotomy

$$\Psi_1(\Psi_2(\Psi_3(U)))$$

$$\Psi_1\Psi_2\Psi_3$$

$$\prod_i \Psi_i$$

Perception is modeled as function composition, where the domain of perception is the Universe. This is depicted in the first equation, where functions operate on the input from earlier functions. Perception is order-dependent: although $f(g(x))$ may sometimes be equivalent to $g(f(x))$, order probably has a slight temporal effect if nothing else. In a linguistic context, such as modifying a noun with multiple adjectives, the order of the adjectives may not matter greatly. In that case, it is possible to model the combination of multiple perceptual operations (or parthood operations) as a mathematical product. Hence, the expressions listed above are equivalent, subject to the implicit presence of some spatial domain in the latter two formulations.

Dichotomy allows for the relatively arbitrary division of percepts: it can operate on percepts because they are spatial and continuous (or at least not atomic).[8] It is essentially a mereological version of intersection: it is different than the set-theoretic definition of intersection, which roughly entails breaking apart a set, choosing some of its members, and then putting them back in a set. In cognitive set theory, as mereology, those steps are explicit. Hence, the operation of dichotomy does not cross set boundaries: only dereferencing, the inverse of the original referencing operation, can deconstruct a set.[9]

Dichotomy can be interpreted as a dividing line which has a dimensionality of one less than the part which it divides. Hence, a line is divided by a point, a surface is divided by a line, etc.

The dividing thing must completely divide the domain. If we take as the domain a plane which extends indefinitely in two dimensions, there are two possibilities for such a dividing line. One is a closed curve within that plane, and the other is an open curve that extends as far as that plane. Both of these curves are dichotomizers, because each of them completely bifurcates the domain.

It is essential to note that the dividing line is not a part of the space that it divides, as it does not take up any space in the domain which it divides. This is due to the fact that points are not seen as composing things, but as dividing them. Similarly, lines should be understood as cuts which divide a continuous plane: they are not things out of which that higher-dimensional continuum can be composed.

11.17: Conception

$$V \equiv \Phi(O)$$

$$x = \Phi_j(O)$$

$$x = \{o_j\}$$

The conceptual universe is composed of references to the subjective universe: these references are called concepts. Concepts are modeled in this book with sets: the formation of a concept is functionally denoted by the operator Φ, and the understanding (or dereferencing) of a concept by Φ^{-1}. As with sets, concepts are also represented using curly braces, {}.

A concept is a reference which is treated as an atomic entity, even though it may represent (i.e. refer to) something with parts. In other words, because a concept is both a set and a reference, it is treated as an atom *in the referring domain*, although it may refer to a continuous element (e.g. a percept) or a (discrete) collection of concepts. Although it is somewhat unconventional to speak of sets as atomic (since they are defined as collections of elements), it is certainly not uncommon to treat them as singular entities: this is exactly what gives them much of their expressive power.

11.18: Collection

$$\{o_1 + o_2 + o_3\}$$

$$\Phi\left(\sum_i o_i\right)$$

The first equation above shows a concept which is a collection of three percepts. The second equation illustrates an alternate notation for the same concept.

As mentioned previously, the dichotomy operator cannot be applied directly to a concept because concepts make their contents atomic (their contents are temporarily opaque). Further, if it were to be applied to a symbol, such as "apple", the result would be something like "app", which is meaningless. In order to allow the formation of subsets, we must first dereference the concept (break apart the set), select certain of its perceptual parts, and then collect these parts into a set. Collection, on the other hand, can only be applied to percepts and symbols (not directly to concepts, as in standard set theory). The result of defining these operators in this way is that all dichotomization (perception) must happen before any collection (conception), unless those concepts are visualized (i.e. their meaning is extracted). This ordering has significant topological consequences which will be explored later.

11.19: Naming

$$O \equiv \varepsilon(V)$$

$$x = \varepsilon(\phi_i)$$

Naming is defined as the association of a concept with an arbitrary percept: its name. Names, or symbols, are parts of the perceptual universe that represent concepts. Hence, their referential level is one higher than the concepts they reference, despite the fact that they are percepts. In virtue of the fact that naming and conception form a loop, percepts and concepts are bound up in mutual reference.

Given a part of the physical universe, it is possible to form a percept which is a reference to it. Given this percept, it is possible to form a concept which is a reference to it. Given this concept, it is possible to again form a percept which is a reference to it. Hence, percepts may reference two very different types of things: in order to distinguish percepts-which-reference-objects from percepts-which-reference-concepts, the latter are called symbols (or names). They are formed using the naming operator, as depicted in the equations above, instead of being formed by perception.

The naming operator has an inverse, whose use is crucial: if we could name concepts, but we could not understand concepts when given their names, names would be of precious little value. We denote this dereferencing operator as the inverse of the naming operator (although it is probably implemented as a separate neural association, since biological inverses pose a tricky implementation problem).

$$y = \varepsilon(x)$$
$$x = \varepsilon^{-1}(y)$$

In the equations above, the naming operator creates a symbol, y, that references a concept, x. The inverse of this operation, which involves recognizing that symbol (i.e. re-cognizing or dereferencing), reactivates the meaning associated with that symbol. In English, the referencing or naming operation relies on the verb *to be*, as in the copula *is* or *is-a*. The dereferencing operation is similarly aided by linguistic constructs: for example, definite and indefinite articles can dereference a count noun, which makes it less abstract.

11.20: Communication

$$u \equiv \Delta(O)$$

$$y_i = \Delta(x_j)$$

The outbound portion of communication entails the creation of objects in the world, such as hieroglyphs and sound waves. This communication may be symbolic or not, depending on the nature of what is being transmitted. If there is no symbolic content, communication may be treated exclusively as action (e.g. as in running). More often, communication is both an action (e.g. the movement of the lips, the movement of the hand) as well as the transmission of symbolic information (the words or the writing that result from this movement).[10]

Topology

The topological notions of connection and overlap are closely related to perception and conception. In particular, the operation of perception can be used to express connection fairly directly: by relying *only* on dichotomy, we can form *only* contiguous percepts. Hence, connection (or contiguity) can be defined as that which can be produced by (multiple operations of) dichotomy in a larger contiguous percept. To express overlap, it is necessary to add collection (since a part of a connected thing is always connected). In other words, in virtue of the way dichotomy and collection are defined, overlapping perception is not possible without introducing naming.

11.21: Connection

$$\text{Connected}(x,y) \triangleq$$

$$\exists z, i \, (x \equiv \{\Psi_i(z)\}) \wedge (y \equiv \{z - \Psi_i(z)\}) \wedge (z \equiv \Pi_j \Psi_j)$$

Two things x and y are connected if and only if they can be represented as a dichotomy of some larger connected (contiguous) z. That larger percept is contiguous because it is derived only from the repeated application of dichotomy to a universe, which is continuous by definition. In particular, that larger thing z must be formed without the use of collection (which would allow z to be a discontiguous entity). In more cognitive terminology, contiguous objects are the result of first perceiving everything, and then restricting attention to smaller parts of that percept (which can be modeled as multiple applications of perceptual intersection).

11.22: Overlap

$$\text{Overlap}(x,y) \triangleq$$
$$\exists\, a,b,c,\ (x \equiv \{a+b\}) \wedge (y \equiv \{b+c\})$$

Two things x and y overlap if and only if they share a part in common (which is denoted as b in the equation above). Both overlap (and underlap, or discontiguous objects) require collection, since dichotomy alone forms only partitions. In other words, the limited scope of dichotomy and collection facilitate the definition of topological connection and overlap. The psychological implications of these topological definitions are somewhat interesting: a single percept must be connected. If overlap (or discontinuity) is required, then concepts (collection) must be used. Intuitively, this seems like a good result; perceptually, objects occlude one another, rather than overlap. Experimentally, this provides a number of testable hypotheses about perception of single and multiple things.

Dimensionality

The ontological universes and the referential relations between them can be used to build increasingly abstract concepts. This abstractness can be quantified in terms of dimensionality. In other words, the following things may be collected into (separate) universes: all things, all things which are references, all things which are references to references, etc. Each of these universes consists of references with a different referential level, and each serves as the basis for a particular point of view.

11.23: Conceptual Order

$$\text{order}(x^n) \triangleq n$$
$$y^{n+1} = \mathcal{E}(x^n)$$

The notion of conceptual order is similar to a concept's level of reference, although it tends to be more convenient. The level of reference of a concept increases with every reference: the order of a concept increases only when a thing is named. For example, if an object is a first-level reference, then a percept is a second-level reference, a concept is a third-level reference, etc. However, if an object is a first-order object, then a percept of that object remains first-order, as does a concept of that percept. It is only when first-order concepts are named that second-order things (symbols) are created. At the same time, the notion of conceptual order still provides a means by which to differentiate percepts that are symbolic from percepts that are not (i.e. percepts which reference objects are always first-order).

The order of a concept corresponds to the number of set braces used in the formation of that concept. The order of a concept assigns to each concept (or set) an integral index (first-order, second-order, etc) which corresponds to its level in the Zermelo hierarchy. There are a number of benefits associated with the Zermelo hierarchy, the most notable of which is that this correspondence goes a long way towards ensuring the well-foundedness of the system. Perhaps more importantly, this notion of order mirrors the way in which our concepts are formed: they are built out of pre-existing percepts and concepts.

11.24: Dimensionality

$$\dim(\text{pt}(x)) \equiv \dim(x)$$
$$\dim(x') \equiv \dim(x') + \text{order}(x')$$

The first equation above states that parts have a dimensionality which is equivalent to the wholes from which they are created. The second equation states that the dimensionality of a concept *x''* is equal to the dimensionality of the underlying percept, x', in addition to any dimensionality added by the conceptual order.

Although the dimensionality of things in a given universe and the dimensionality of that universe itself are equivalent, universes do not necessarily have the same dimensionality as each other. For example, references often have a dimensionality which differs from the things they reference. Clearly, this is only true when they are understood *as* references: as parts, they exist in the same universe as the things they refer to, so in that context they necessarily have the same dimensionality as the things they reference.

The collection of multiple concepts enables an increase in dimensionality: the new dimension is a dimension of variation over the collected things. Since the things are atomic (as references), this collection is necessarily orthogonal to the things themselves: it is one-dimensional. Contrast this with a three-dimensional thing, which could only be combined with other three-dimensional things.[11]

There are two points of view with respect to the dimensionality of collected concepts. From one point of view, if each of the collected parts has a dimensionality of N, then by collecting them together, we have created a thing of dimension (N+1). From another point of view, as the collected things are atomic, the result is a one-dimensional collection. The difference between these points of view amounts to whether or not the concepts thus collected are dereferenced in the process of considering their dimensionality.[12]

11.25: Hierarchy

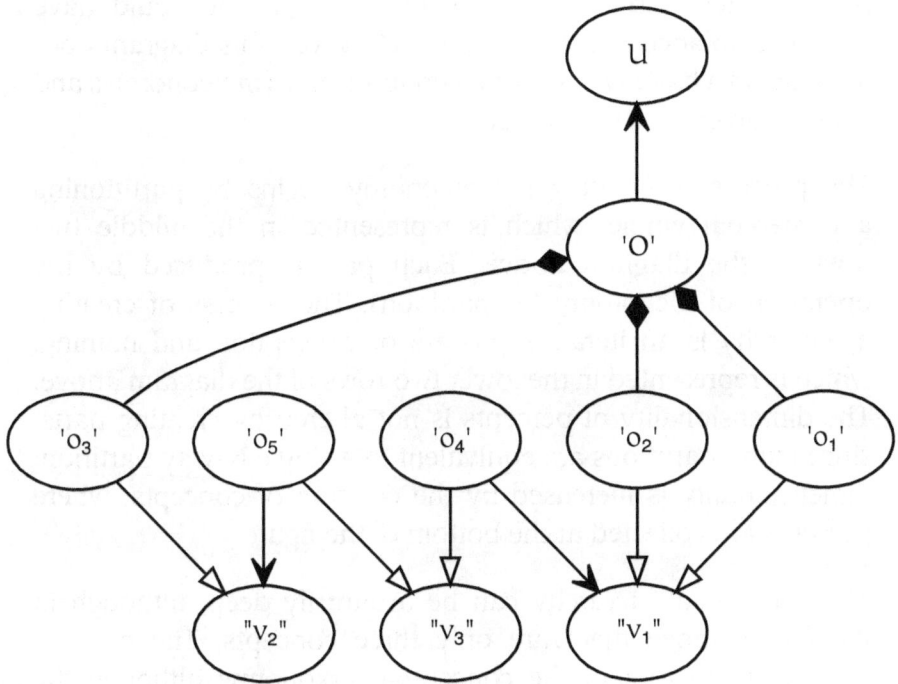

The diagram above shows several example relations between things in all three universes. At the top level, the Universe (U) is depicted: this is reflected into the perceptual universe (O), and subsequently divided into the percepts 'o_1', 'o_2', and 'o_3'. This perceptual hierarchy is a trivial example of a meronomy, or part-hierarchy (this is indicated by the diamond arrowheads). At the next level of the diagram, these percepts are referenced by the concepts "v_1" and "v_2". These concepts unify their corresponding percepts, and each has a corresponding symbol or name: 'o_4' and 'o_5'. Finally, those names are collected into a single higher-order concept, "v_3".

It is important to note that this diagram has deceptively clean lines: it is a misleadingly simple hierarchy, represented here with several symbolic nodes. While this simplicity is useful to visualize things, it is misleading in that the underlying implementation is distributed and considerably more tangled: it would have little resemblance to these pictures. However, this diagram does illustrate in a basic way how perception creates mereonomies and conception creates taxonomies.

The process of creating a mereonomy begins by partitioning a perceptual whole, which is represented in the middle two rows of the diagram above. Each part is produced by the operation of dichotomy (or partition). The process of creating a hierarchy is an iterative process of conception and naming, which is represented in the lower two rows of the diagram above. The dimensionality of percepts is not altered by creating parts, since many partitions are equivalent to a single N-way partition: dimensionality is increased by the creation of concepts, where percepts are collected at the bottom of the figure.

The conceptual hierarchy can be arbitrarily deep, although in the figure above there are only three concepts. The concept "v_3" is at the root of the conceptual taxonomy: although the existence of a single conceptual root is not necessary, it has an interesting correspondence to the perceptual universe (O).[13] It should be clear from the pictures that there are multiple ways to derive a concept such as "v_3" which ultimately corresponds to the perceptual universe (O). None of these derivations is more correct than another: although they may be expressed differently symbolically, they mean the same thing.

To understand this diagram better, we may give the nodes a familiar interpretation. Let us suppose that this diagram represents a world which consists of only one dog and one cat. We have not divided the physical universe into the dog and the cat; instead, we perceive the entire world, and we form concepts ("v_1" and "v_2") based on seeing the dog once ('o_3') and the cat twice ('o_1', 'o_2'). Further, we learn the names for cat and dog ('o_4' and 'o_5', perhaps 'Felix' and 'Canus'). We think that Felix is something, and that Canus is something, but we do not have a word for that something (i.e. a name for the concept "v_3"). If we were to name it, it would probably be something like 'animal'.

Identity

Identity is one of the most basic relations. In order to define identity, we begin with a situation in which nothing is identical with anything else: everything is unique unto itself. All perceptions are different: however, these different perceptions may be collected into concepts (and thus unitized). At that point, differences between individual percepts can be ignored or forgotten. It is in virtue of this forgetting that different percepts become identical (at least from the conceptual point of view).

There are several kinds of identity to consider, based on the relationship of different kinds of things to one another. For example, the identity conditions for parts are somewhat different than for references (at least when references are treated *as* references). We begin with the notion of identity between two things in the same universe.

11.26: Identity

$$(x \equiv y) \triangleq ID_{intrinsic}(x, y) \wedge ID_{extrinsic}(x, y)$$

Two objects within the same universe are identical (or are the same thing) if they are both intrinsically and extrinsically identical.

11.27: Intrinsic Identity

$$ID_{intrinsic}(x, y) \triangleq \forall z, z \subset x \leftrightarrow z \subset y$$

The equation of intrinsic identity states that two things are equal if and only if they are composed of the same parts.

11.28: Extrinsic Identity

$$ID_{extrinsic}(x, y) \triangleq \forall z, x \subset z \leftrightarrow y \subset z$$

The equation of extrinsic identity states that two sets are equal if and only if they are both parts of all larger wholes of which either one is a part.

11.29: Referential Identity

$$\text{ID}_{\text{referential}}(x^n, y^m) \triangleq \text{ID}_{\text{refEq}}(x^{n-1}, y^{m-1})$$

$$\text{ID}_{\text{refEq}}(x^n, y^m) \triangleq (x \equiv y) \lor \text{ID}_{\text{refEq}}(x^{n-1}, y^{m-1})$$

Two references are *referentially identical* if they refer to the same thing. This entails that x and y are references, and that after some amount of dereferencing, they are identical to one another non-referentially. The notion of identity itself is not sufficient (as an identity condition) for references, because two different references are always different as things. On one hand, this outcome is desirable because we need a way to say that two references are not equivalent. However, we also need a way to say when references, which are not themselves identical, refer to the same thing (i.e. $\text{ref}^1(x) \equiv \text{ref}^1(y)$).

11.30: Isomorphic Identity

$$(x \cong y) \triangleq (x \cong_{\text{int}} y) \land (x \cong_{\text{ext}} y)$$

$$(x \cong_{\text{int}} y) \triangleq \forall\, w \exists\, z,\, (w \subset x \to z \subset y) \land (w \cong z)$$

$$(x \cong_{\text{ext}} y) \triangleq \forall\, w \exists\, z,\, (x \subset w \to y \subset z) \land (w \cong z)$$

Isomorphic identity establishes identity between references and the things that they reference (i.e. their referents). Isomorphic identity implies both extrinsic and intrinsic isomorphism. This entails that a reference is isomorphic to its referent if and only if both participate in the same extrinsic and intrinsic relations in their respective domains.

Isomorphism is guaranteed between a referential universe (a full set) and the universe to which it refers (at least when both things are regarded as undifferentiated). In other words, all full sets are isomorphic to one another: both their intrinsic and their extrinsic identity is trivially satisfied since they are both universes as well as atoms. For parts which are created from these universes, isomorphism requires structural similarity: a reference is isomorphic to its referent if everything of which they are parts are also isomorphic to each other.

Logic

11.31: Classical Logic

$$y = vx$$

$$y = v(1 - x)$$

$$vy = vx$$

$$vy = v(1 - x)$$

George Boole's fantastic work entitled "The Laws of Thought" stated Aristotle's four syllogisms using the concise formulation shown above. In these equations, the letter v is used to express the concept of "some" (which we interpret as being synonymous with parthood), the numeral one (1) is used to represent truth, and zero (0) is used to indicate falsity. These laws have mereological counterparts which can be written in a straightforward manner as follows:

Aristotelian Syllogisms	Mereological Equations
All y are x	$y = pt(x)$
No y are x	$y = pt(\neg x)$
Some y are x	$pt(y) = pt(x)$
Some y are not x	$pt(y) = pt(\neg x)$

These mereological equations can be easily visualized with Venn diagrams. For example, the first statement (in which all y's are x's), can be represented as a circle around all of the y's, inside of a circle around all of the x's. All of these representations are mereological formalisms which are *complementary* to the existential quantification over individuals (i.e. we do not attempt to replace mereology with set theory).

11.32: Existential Quantifiers
Rectangles are polygons.

$\forall\, x, x \in \text{Rect} \rightarrow x \in \text{Poly}$

$\text{Rect } \varepsilon \text{ pt}(\text{Poly}(U))$

$\text{Rect } \varepsilon \text{ Equilateral}(\text{Poly}(U))$

Modern logic transforms the first statement above into the second statement with the use of existential quantifiers. As can be seen, existential quantifiers reduce abstract propositions to concrete propositions that range over (less abstract) individuals. While this is often a useful transformation, it cannot be the whole story from a cognitive perspective. A psychological version of set theory must allow direct expression of higher-order statements, i.e. statements which are not about individuals, but abstract things. Instead of using quantification over entities, which is a limitation imposed by first-order predicate calculus, abstract logical statements must be able to relate to one another directly. This is done in the third equation, which says that rectangles are types of polygons (where we have interpreted a type as an abstract part). In even more detail, rectangles are the part of polygons that are equilateral, which is expressed in equation four.

When it comes to expressing English in a formal language, the goal of logicians is not the same as the goal of psychologists. Logicians must be conservative with respect to the introduction of axioms. Psychologists, on the other hand, must respect the operating principles of the mind and the brain, even if those principles turn out to be somewhat redundant. For example, logicians might regard the sentence "Rectangles are polygons" as identical in deep structure to the sentence "Every rectangle is a polygon", or even "Every thing which is a rectangle is a thing which is a polygon". Although these statements may be logically equivalent under certain conditions, they are not equivalent from a cognitive point of view. For example, if quantification over all individuals were required to reach a conclusion, conclusions would take a good deal longer to reach.

If we allow for different cognitive structures corresponding to the sentences in the left-hand column, we might end up with the following table, where the order of the concepts involved in the relation is indicated in the third column:

English	Cognitive Structure	Order
Rectangles are polygons	$R \, \varepsilon \, P$	second
Every rectangle is a polygon	$\forall x : r(x) \rightarrow p(x)$	first
Every thing which is a rectangle is a thing which is a polygon	$\forall x : x \in R \rightarrow x \in P$	first

The quantification required by first-order logic relies on individuals and the existence of individuals. Hence, existential quantification works well for things which can be easily individuated, such as count nouns. It is awkward when applied to mass nouns, as in "water is wet", where we are forced to read $\forall w$ as "for all waters w". Those concrete individuals must exist in order to be meaningful. This means that if there are no individuals satisfying the premise $r(x)$ in the second equation above (i.e. no rectangles), then the implication is true for the first-order sentences. On the other hand, the second-order version of the statement can be false even in a world without rectangles. In other words, actual rectangles are not required for the second-order formulation: we may infer the truth or falsity of statements from these second-order terms, independently of any individuals.[14]

Linguistics

The meaning of words derives from concepts, which in turn have a meaning that depends on the original contextual embedding of the percepts from which those concepts are ultimately formed. Syntax governs the combination of these semantic units; it is a referential calculus which organizes concepts in a high-dimensional space, and which provides a listener with rules to dereference the encoded meaning of various utterances by a speaker.

The deep structure of language and the study of syntax are crucial parts of cognitive set theory. However, there are two significant differences between cognitive set theory and syntactic structure. The first way in which cognitive set theory differs is with respect to its scope: by attempting to describe perception, and to a lesser extent reality, the modeling attempted in cognitive set theory extends beyond the range of syntax and semantics.

The second way in which cognitive set theory differs significantly from syntactic theory is that it recognizes two distinct kinds of syntax (or at least, an additional top-level production rule). These two types of syntax correspond to two types of sentences, those expressing an event and those expressing a relation. The first type is well-characterized by traditional binary-branching syntax and consists, at the highest syntactic level, of the combination of a noun phrase and a verb phrase. The second type of sentence creates an identity relation between two things (as opposed to constituting a reference to a thing). Although this second type of sentence arguably shares the same syntactic rules, is so radically different from other sentences at a cognitive level that it warrants a special treatment.

11.33: Properties

$$\exists x, x \in \text{Cats} \wedge P_{\text{black}}(x)$$

$$\exists x, P_{\text{cat}}(x) \wedge x \in \text{BlackThings}$$

$$\exists x, x \in \text{Cats} \wedge x \in \text{BlackThings}$$

$$\exists x, P_{\text{cat}}(x) \wedge P_{\text{black}}(x)$$

Consider the phrase "black cats". Syntactically, this phrase is an adjective followed by a noun. Logically, both "black" and "cats" can be rendered with either properties (which the denoted entity has) or sets (of which the denoted entity is a member). The four possibilities for rendering this phrase are shown in the equations above. The first equation above is similar to the English sentence, where "cat" is a noun and "black" is a property. The second equation depicts "cat" as a property and "black" as a thing (a concrete individual). The third equation is especially amenable to an extensional set-theoretic interpretation, since it deals exclusively with entities and set membership. The fourth equation is expressed entirely in terms of properties: it is very close to a mereological formulation. A mereological point of view, however, does not need to quantify over entities, and may therefore be written as:

$$P_{\text{black}}(P_{\text{cats}}(U))$$

This rendering, precisely because it does not quantify over individuals, is what makes mereology such an attractive logic for dealing with shapes, substances, and other (potentially continuous) spatial things which do not come in neat and tidy (individualized) packages. It is attractive because it can be expressed without quantification (which has the side effect of dereferencing, or reducing the dimensionality, of the expression). In other words, by applying quantifiers to things (*there exists a* cat, or *the* cat), we make those things more concrete (or less abstract). While this may be necessary in order to refer to things in the world, it is problematic given that our original phrase was "black cats" instead of "the black cats".

11.34: Nouns as Applied Adjectives
$$\Psi_{green}(\Psi_{tomato}(U))$$

Nouns and adjectives are quite similar, despite the fact that they are different parts of speech: conceptually, "green tomatoes" and "tomatoey green-things" are approximately equivalent (at least denotationally). In both of these phrases, adjectives modify nouns: the English language requires a noun in subject position for proper interpretation. In cognitive set theory, the underlying cognitive structure of a noun essentially contains an adjective (this should be understood at a deep level, since it is clearly not true at the surface level). In other words, both nouns and adjectives are composed of the same cognitive operation. Nouns are essentially adjectives which have been applied (to space). Given this understanding, the cognitive structure of equation 11.34 can be represented as follows:

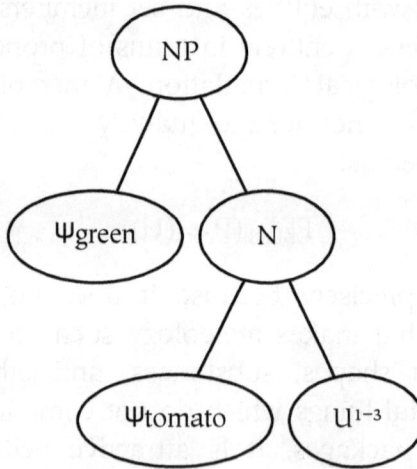

Figure 11.1: The Cognitive Structure of Nouns

This structure illustrates that nouns are parts of speech which are themselves compound. For example, the noun "tomato" may be written as $\Psi_{tomato}(U^{1-3})$, which may be understood in a manner analogous an adjective which has been applied to a space. Although treating nouns as *pre-applied adjectives* cannot be argued from the surface structure of English, this transformation simplifies the underlying cognitive processes. For one thing, having fewer cognitive structures than parts of speech is desirable, as it is unlikely that there are different mental mechanisms for all of the different parts of speech. By allowing the different parts of speech to share a common deep structure, they can be modeled in a uniform way. For example, just as noun phrases may be constructed out of adjectives and nouns, nouns themselves may be (implicitly) constructed from adjectives.[15] Similarly, verbs can be modeled as adverbs which have been applied to a conceptual space. As opposed to noun phrases, however, the conceptual space upon which verbs operate is time (U^4).

11.35: Statements Expressing Relations

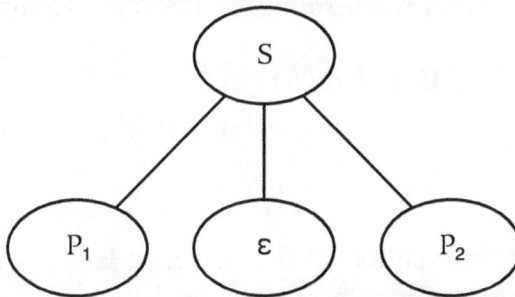

Statements which express a relation have their own production rule in cognitive set theory, which is depicted above. This is done to illustrate that these statements are *categorically* different from sentences using the production rule that divides a sentence into a noun phrase and a verb phrase. Even if syntactically we wish to preserve the traditional binary-branching tree structure, sentences expressing relations should be recognized as radically different from a cognitive perspective.

At a high level, the syntax of a sentence expressing a relation is modeled with three parts: a concept (such as the symbol which is to be defined), a copula (represented by epsilon), and a second concept (which provides the definition). Although there are numerous types of relations, all of them can be reduced to this ternary form. [16] The epsilon symbol is the relation that represents naming, and corresponds in English to some form of the verb *to be*. The operation of naming does not always introduce the name for the first time: it may only refine the definition of an existing symbol. However, in order to keep the presentation simple, we will consider the case in which the thing on the left is completely defined by (or becomes a name for) the thing on the right.

In order to illustrate the construction used to define new words, we consider the following phrase, where (D) represents "Dorsochimps", (s) represents "small", (m) represents "meddlesome", and (a) represents "animals":

"Dorsochimps are small, meddlesome animals".

$$D \; \varepsilon \; s(m(a))$$
$$D(U^{1\text{-}3}) \; \varepsilon \; s(m(a(U^{1\text{-}3})))$$
$$D(U^{1\text{-}3}) \; \varepsilon \; ms(a(U^{1\text{-}3}))$$

The symbolic formulation of the sentence is shown in the first of the equations above. In the second equation, the nouns are modeled in the same way as adjectives which have been applied to an (implicit) concept of space (which we have represented with the symbol $U^{1\text{-}3}$). Finally, in the third equation, intersection is used instead of function composition, under the assumption that the order of application does not make a significant difference for the adjective "meddlesome". "Small", however, must be understood in the context of animals, so it is not subject to this treatment.

An important characteristic of this sentence is that time does not enter the picture: this sentence expresses a relation between abstract entities. Even though this sentence possesses a verb, it is atemporal (or eternal), which is a common characteristic of relations. In other words, relations are independent of time, since they define abstract concepts. The ultimate result of this definition is the association of a new word ("dorsochimps") with its meaning. This previously unknown symbol is tied to a single compound concept (using the operation of naming). A slightly more complicated definition would entail the collection of multiple concepts. For example, we might wish to say that dorsochimps are both small, meddlesome animals *and* things which often travel in packs (which requires the operation of collection).

11.36: Statements Expressing Things

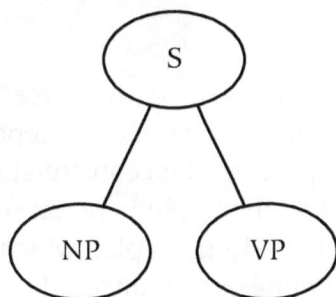

In addition to sentences which express relations, there are also sentences which express things, or events in the world. As an example, consider a person reading the following sentence:

The apple from that tree probably tasted good.

This sentence is about the world. It is communicated as a series of symbols, so the underlying concept must be unpacked through successive operations of perception, conception, and understanding (the inverse of naming). Here we will conduct a basic syntactic analysis of the sentence to illustrate how it can be constructed as a single high-dimensional event.

At the first syntactic division, the sentence is a combination of a noun phrase and a verb phrase. The sentence structure can be broken down slightly further as follows:

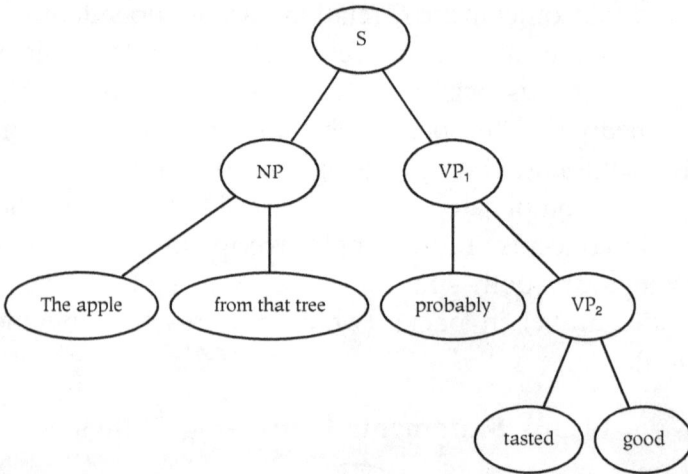

The noun phrase "The apple from that tree" is a dynamically-constructed concept (or an unnamed concept), as is every node in the tree during the process of its construction.[17] The subject of the sentence is "apple": the apple is represented as an abstract count noun (a four-dimensional apple), which was at some point defined in terms of a number of individual apple concepts (each of which is a three-dimensional apple). The four-dimensional "apple-from-that-tree" is indexed by the use of the definite article. In so doing, the associated concept changes from an abstract count noun back to a dynamically-constructed concrete noun: the (three-dimensional) "the-apple-from-that-tree". The modification of the noun by the phrase "from that tree" does not alter the dimensionality of the thing, but it does refine the concept; it restricts the set of "apples" to the more restricted set of "apples on that tree".

At this point, the concept corresponding to the (three-dimensional) noun phrase, the-apple-from-that-tree, can be joined with the verb phrase, "probably tasted good". The modifier "probably" specifies the location of the thing on a modal dimension. In more philosophical terminology, of all of the possible and actual worlds, this modifier conveys that there is a significant probability that the thing which is being referred to occupies *this* world.

The rest of the verb phrase consists of a transitive verb and its object, "tasted" and "good". The verb phrase adds a temporal dimension to the thing described; in this example, a previous time frame is indicated by the use of past tense.[18] The verb "taste" is itself abstract in virtue of the fact that it is transitive; it requires an additional part (the object of the sentence) before it can become a well-formed reference. In other words, "tasted-x" is a verb phrase which is itself essentially two-dimensional: the addition of the (required) modifier turns the verb phrase into a one-dimensional (temporal) concept.

The sentence refers to an object (i.e. a high-dimensional event). The constituent phrases each specify the nature of the object along different dimensions. The noun phrase is responsible for three spatial dimensions, and the verb phrase is responsible for modal and temporal dimensions. Collecting these together, we have a five-dimensional specification of a thing. In other words, the sentence is rendered as a five-dimensional event: three of which are spatial, one of which is temporal, and one of which is modal (i.e. associated with some probability of occurrence). This concept is communicated in written form. The process of communication entails the formation of the individual symbols corresponding to the constituent concepts, which are then communicated to the world through the inscription of the symbols on the printed page.

Through this communication, an object is created in the world: a series of typewritten characters. Although they are clearly a part of the physical universe and not concepts themselves, they have symbolic significance. The reader may retrieve the symbolic meaning from this perceived sentence through the reverse of the process just described. Critically important to this endeavor is to make the assumption that there *is* symbolic significance to the words that you are reading in the first place. You must believe that this inscription corresponds to a valid concept, otherwise

you would be content to have merely perceived it, as opposed to
having understood it.

Notes

[1]This story is changing, however: mereology is returning to the limelight of intellectual thought.

[2]Dereferencing a reference may result in *multiple things*: in this context, that would allow multiple entities on either side of the equivalence operator.

[3]In logic, the typical use of negation connotes that it is productive of a new truth. Since we view negation to be an inescapable result of dichotomy (or the parthood operation), it should be viewed as a method of referring to a pre-existing object. It is often used as a convenience to address the case in which we don't wish to name the object on both sides of a decision boundary. Its use implies that we know the domain of discourse: for logical operations, the domain of discourse is simply true or false. More generally, the negation operator can represent a mereological or set complement operation.

Sometimes the domain of discourse is implicit. For example, imagine the domain of "not fish": it seems plausible that a bird is "not fish", but it seems less plausible that the color green is "not fish". In this case, the domain of discourse seems to be partially determined by the spatial characteristics of "not fish".

[4]Failure to recognize this essential characteristic leads to a great misunderstanding of set theory. However, removing this boundary creates a logic closely related to mereology: from the mereological point of view, there is no difference between a thing and a part which contains all of that thing. In more psychological terms, there is no ontological reality to the set braces.

[5]One difficulty with the element-of operator (for our purposes) is that it is not constructive. We follow the convention of defining a left-hand side from a pre-defined right hand side, and we hold that elements must exist before a collection of those elements. Hence, the element-of operator cannot be used to constructively define new sets. It is perhaps unnecessary that the relation is constructive for mathematics, where it can be used simply as a relation. However, since we want to model cognition, and we view cognition as something which builds concepts out of other things, it makes sense to use only constructive axioms.

Unfortunately, the construction that we provide in the second equation is a bit more cumbersome than the equation which uses the element-of operation. However, this notational inconvenience is worth the benefit of an explicit (functional) formalism to represent curly braces.

[6]The use of an epsilon, ε, to denote naming is motivated by its use in the work of Lesniewski, where it has a very definite linguistic role (is-a). It should not be confused with the lunate epsilon (element) operation of set theory, or the extension operator of Hilbert. In fact, it is very similar to the inverse of Hilbert's epsilon (at one point in the writing of this book naming was written as a backwards epsilon, but that caused insurmountable typographical issues).

Lesniewski's system, called ontology, does not use sets, and set theory does not use the naming operator. In cognitive set theory, these two logical systems are conjoined by treating the following equations as synonymous:

$$\alpha = \{\beta\}$$

$$\alpha \, \varepsilon \, \beta$$

[7]Topology finds itself in the awkward position of having to decide to which part of a divided whole the dividing line belongs. For this reason, cognitive set theory holds that the dividing line itself does not exist in the domain that it divides, much as a knife edge is not a part of the sandwich it cuts in half.

[8]We characterize percepts as continuous in light of the fact that they are continuous in comparison to concepts: whether they are ultimately continuous in a mathematical sense is somewhat irrelevant here.

[9]Although both continuous things and discrete collections can have a partition, atoms cannot. For example:

- Continuous things can be partitioned, such as an apple or the percept of an 'apple'.

- Discrete *collections* can be partitioned, such as coins (even if coins are atomic). Similarly, the collections of concepts (that represent these things individually) can be partitioned.

- Atoms themselves cannot be partitioned: if they could, it would imply that the atoms had parts. Since concepts are atomic, the concept of an apple cannot be partitioned (without first casting that concept into a perceptual space).

[10]We are presuming that the physical universe is itself void of symbolic (referential) content, but that it may always be interpreted symbolically (referentially) by an observer. However, it may be the case that the world is never without meaning, in which case action without communication is impossible.

[11]It is an interesting question how dimensionality might be represented in the brain, because we have stated that the dimensionality of references is not equivalent to the dimensionality of the things which are referenced. Note that dimensional considerations are not an issue for concepts: since concepts are characterized as atomic entities, they do not have any dimensional constraints. The removal of these constraints allows concepts of arbitrary dimensionality to be collected in a one-dimensional space. The question of dimensionality is more interesting for perception, since the dimensionality of the world may be greater or lesser than the actual dimensionality of the representation in our brains, and perception maintains a (spatial) metric structure.

Neural encoding of dimensionality may be related to interconnectedness. For example, dimensionality can be approximately expressed as the number of neighbors shared by an atom: an element in a one dimensional space has exactly two neighbors, one to each side of itself on the line. Similarly, an element in a two dimensional space has four neighbors (assuming that neighbors are arranged in a Euclidean grid, and that one does not count the neighbors that can be reached diagonally). Following this line of thought further, an N-dimensional space can be produced by connecting each atom to 2^N of its neighbors (in a regular fashion).

[12]We adopt the convention that concepts are always of a greater dimension than the percepts they reference (from a more mathematical point of view, we would say that the dimensionality increases, but the rank does not).

This convention is not a problem for collections, since there really is a dimension over which the individual concepts vary (i.e. the range of summation). For count nouns such as an apple, therefore, an increase in dimensionality will not come as a surprise: the formation of a count noun implies a concept with an extension that ranges over a plurality of instances. However, it is a bit puzzling for sets which consist of exactly one entity. Is a concept that corresponds to a single individual (i.e. the concept behind a proper noun) really of a higher dimensionality than the object which it names? Is it not just a reference to the latter? In this case, the dimension (even if it does exist) is not a proper dimension, but it is still treated as a dimension for uniformity with other (proper) dimensions.

[13]Note that "v_3" is not equivalent to the conceptual universe (V), which in this case would have to include "v_{1-2}".

[14]It would be interesting to remove existential quantifiers entirely. For the existence operator, doing so is not difficult: for example, if we have a sentence such as "There exists a thing which is both a rectangle and a polygon", we may render it logically as follows:

$$\exists x : r(x) \wedge p(x)$$

$$\{ \, r(U) \, p(U) \, \} \neq \varnothing$$

For the $\forall$ operator, however, this is harder to do. In particular, it is not clear how to remove quantification from the equations for intrinsic and extrinsic identity.

[15]Again, it is clearly not the case that adjectives are nouns, or vice-versa: they are very distinct things. However, nouns and adjectives share the same type of abstract cognitive operation in that they restrict space: adjectives are abstract because they have not yet been applied to a spatial entity, and nouns are concrete exactly because they have been applied to a spatial entity. In functional terms, the domain of adjectives is the noun, and the domain of nouns is space itself (although the latter is implicit in the English language).

We are not merely arguing that sharing a single cognitive implementation makes our lives simpler as psychologists. Reducing the complexity of the neural mechanisms which explain speech and language is justified in virtue of the fact that our brains, despite their enormous complexity, probably did not suddenly evolve lots of different mechanisms simultaneously to handle the different parts of speech. The ability to use most, if not all, parts of speech evolved more or less at once, so having only one underlying mechanism seems likely.

[16]Syntax decomposes sentences into noun phrases and verb phrases, while logic decomposes sentences into entities and relations. Logical relations are sometimes considered to be more powerful than binary branching syntax, but this is not the case. Expressions in either form can be re-written as expressions in the other: consider the relation "loves" in the phrase "Alec loves the girl". Under a logical analysis, we may write this as follows:

$$loves(Alec, \text{the girl})$$

Under a syntactic analysis, we may break this sentence into a noun phrase and a verb phrase:

$$loves\text{-the-girl}(Alec)$$

On the surface, this sentence is different from the first sentence. However, this can be further analyzed into the following part structure, which is very similar to the first:

$$loves(\text{the-girl})(Alec)$$

However, although these sentences *can* be transformed from one to the other, these transformations should be done with caution. These different structures may map onto very different meanings: we may view the fact that "Alec is a girl-lover" as a part of the definition of Alec, or as in "Alec currently loves the girl" (which is clearly a statement of affairs:).

[17]Although two concepts are not be able to be conceived at the same time, concepts can certainly occur successively, and two successive concepts whose names are known can be replaced by a concept which represents their union. Through this process, concepts can be created dynamically by successive union in a sentential hierarchy with a binary-branching syntax.

[18]In one sense, the verb phrase contributes a new dimension of analysis to the thing being conceived. On the other hand, if we consider a three dimensional thing to be really an unchanging four-dimensional thing, then we have not added any dimensionality, but have instead modified that unchanging thing (i.e. changed the shape of the object in the fourth dimension).

Chapter 12: Epilogue

Now this is not the end. It is not even the beginning of the end. But it is, perhaps, the end of the beginning. - Winston Churchill

●　●　●

This book presents a number of features of cognition, many of which are explained using concepts from set theory and mereology. Its aim is to contribute to our understanding of ourselves and the world: to do so, it touches on numerous fields such as psychology, mereology, mathematics, philosophy, and linguistics. As it has collected together subject matter from a wide range of topics, it has been somewhat necessary to avoid going into great depth. If you would like to know more, please visit the companion website at http://www.cognitivesettheory.com

On a personal note, I hope that reading this book has been both enjoyable and intellectually stimulating. I apologize for any mistakes I have made or any ignorance I have unwittingly transmitted.

May it benefit all beings.

Appendix A: The Root Text

· **Part 1: Things** In a general sense, there are three types of objects: everythings, somethings, and nothings. In a universe, there can exist only one everything, many somethings, and exactly zero nothings.

  · **Chapter 1.1: Everything** Everything means every thing, taken together. Although it may be conceptualized as a single unit, it is best to regard everything as something which is neither singular nor plural (because the concept of singularity requires the concept of plurality).

    · **1.1.1: The Whole** Everything cannot be defined.

      · **A Definition of Everything** Everything occupies every position in all dimensions which are attributed to it.

      · **The Properties of Everything** Everything neither has properties nor has no properties.

    · **1.1.2: Universes** Universes are everything from a particular point of view.

    · **1.1.3: The Integrity of Wholes** Wholes, as opposed to collections of parts, are united.

  · **Chapter 1.2: Something** Something is the result of partitioning a larger thing.

    · **1.2.1: Parts** The partition of a thing and the parts of that thing entail one another.

    · **1.2.2: Atoms** The smallest thing has no parts.

      · **Parts of Reduced Dimensionality** Something cannot have a dimensionality less than its parent thing; it occupies a nonzero interval on every dimension which the parent occupies.

- **1.2.3: Properties** The properties of something may be extrinsic or intrinsic. All objects have extrinsic properties except everything, and all objects have intrinsic properties except atoms.

  - **Intrinsic Properties** Intrinsic properties characterize the parts of a thing.

  - **Extrinsic Properties** Extrinsic properties characterize the whole of which a thing is a part.

  - **Relativistic Properties** Properties characterize the relations of a thing.

- **1.2.4: Dichotomy** Dichotomy both collectivizes and dichotomizes, without being intrusive on the dichotomized domain.

  - **Sets and Wholes** Sets are discrete: they may be divided into their members in only one way. Wholes are continuous: they may be divided into further parts in arbitrary ways.

  - **Boundaries** A universe has no boundaries

  - **Truth, Falsity, and Everything in Between** True and false are the essence of categorization.

- **1.2.5: Dimensions** Dimensions are an extension of the concept of dichotomy.

  - **Nominal** Nominal dimensions have unordered parts.

  - **Ordinal** Ordinal dimensions are nominal dimensions that have an associated order.

- **Interval** Interval dimensions are ordinal dimensions that have an associated measure.

- **1.2.6: Hierarchy** A hierarchy is a structure corresponding to successive partitions of a thing.

  - **Ontological Priority** As concepts occupy positions in ontological hierarchies with a single root, the notion of ontological priority is introduced.

  - **Constructing Dimensions** The number of dimensions of a thing is conceptually increased by iterating something along a singleton dimension.

- **Chapter 1.3: Nothing** Nothing is a reference which does not refer to something.

  - **1.3.1: Nothing** Nothing is the complement of everything

  - **1.3.2: References** References form the basis for points of view.

    - **Notational and Denotational Equivalence** References may differ, even though the things they refer to are the same.

    - **Encoding Information** References encode small amounts of information about the referenced domain.

  - **1.3.3: Existence** Existence refers to the possibility of validly dereferencing concepts.

  - **1.3.4: Identity** For two things to be called the same thing implies the notion of identity.

    - **Spatial Identity** Knowing a thing's identity requires knowing the spatial boundaries of that thing.

- **Temporal Identity** Knowing a thing's identity requires knowing the temporal boundaries of that thing.

- **Referential Identity** Two references are referentially identical if they have the same referent.

- **Isomorphic Identity** A reference has a valid correspondence to a referenced thing if their respective relations in each universe are identical.

- **Part 2: Universes** There are three well-known universes: the objective universe, the perceptual universe, and the conceptual universe.

  - **Chapter 2.1: The Physical Universe** All things are parts of the physical universe.

    - **2.1.1: Dimensions of the Physical Universe** The dimensions most commonly attributed to the physical world are the three spatial and the temporal.

      - **The Nature of the Physical Dimensions** The physical dimensions are most often conceived to be Euclidean.

    - **2.1.2: Parts of the Physical Universe** The parts of the physical universe are called objects.

      - **Primitives of Reality: Spatial Things versus Events** All objects occupy a nonzero interval of time.

    - **2.1.3: The Subjective/Objective Dichotomy** The division between the subjective and the objective defines life.

      - **2.1.3.1: The Objective Domain** The objective domain consists of those things which are not referential.

- **Causation** The actions of lifeless things are determined from the outside.

- **2.1.3.2: The Subjective Domain** The subjective domain consists of those things which, for some individual, refer to things in the physical universe.

  - **The Source of Volition** Living things are described as having a choice.

- **Chapter 2.2: The Subjective Universe** The subjective universe is the part of the physical universe that is directly perceived by a single individual.

  - **2.2.1: Dimensions of the Subjective Universe** The most common partition of the subjective universe involves five external and several internal senses, which together form a nominal dimension.

    - **External Perception** The dimensionality and mapping of the various sensory modalities is sense-specific.

    - **Internal Perception** Internal perception is responsible for like and dislike.

  - **2.2.2: Parts of the Subjective Universe** All of our experience comes to us through our external and internal senses.

    - **Perceptual Correspondence** Percepts are formed of both objects and concepts.

    - **Spatial and Temporal Parts** Perception is perception of change.

    - **Attention** Awareness may be restricted to parts of certain dimensions.

- **2.2.3: The Conceptual/Perceptual Dichotomy** A concept is a reference to a part of subjective experience, or a generalization of percepts.

  - **2.2.3.1: The Perceptual Domain** The perceptual domain is composed of perception: it includes sensation, excludes conception, and consists of references to objective reality.

  - **2.2.3.2: The Conceptual Domain** The conceptual domain is composed of things called concepts, which are references to percepts.

    - **Definition of a Concept** Concepts are categories of percepts which are the result of partitioning something.

- **Chapter 2.3: The Conceptual Universe** The conceptual universe is the domain of language.

  - **2.3.1: Dimensions of the Conceptual Universe** First-order concepts refer to percepts, which refer to objects; they derive their semantic value [meaning] from that which they reference and their relationship to other references.

    - **Decision Boundaries** Concepts unify the perceptual data on one side of a decision boundary.

    - **Intuition** A picture is worth a thousand words.

  - **2.3.2: Parts of the Conceptual Universe** The parts of the conceptual universe are called concepts.

    - **2.3.2.1: The Sentence** The smallest valid reference in the conceptual universe is the sentence.

- **2.3.2.2: The Noun Phrase** The noun phrase identifies the spatial extent of sentences.

  - **The First Concepts** The primary notion of identity is called self-identity.

  - **Self/Other** The primary notion of identity is called self-identity.

  - **Proper, Mass, and Count Nouns** Different types of nouns are abstracted from events in different ways, in virtue of which they require different quantifiers.

  - **Ontological Priority of Nouns** The abstractness of nouns can be quantified by using the notions of dimensionality and conceptual order.

- **2.3.2.3: The Verb Phrase** The verb phrase is the temporal part of sentences about events.

  - **Transitive and Intransitive Verbs** Verb phrases may be intransitive, in which case the verbs are semantically complete, or transitive, in which case the verbs require an object.

- **Part 3: References** References are relations which are capable of bridging universes.

- **Chapter 3.1: Subjective/Objective References** Between the objective domain and the subjective domain are two primary relationships: perception and communication.

  - **3.1.1: Perception** Perception is that process by which objects in the objective world are represented by percepts in the subjective world of an individual.

- **Bottom-up Perception** Percepts are caused, to some degree, by the objects that they reference.

- **Top-down Perception** Percepts are caused, to some degree, by the mind in which they occur.

- **3.1.2: Communication** Communication is that process by which events in the subjective world of an individual are represented in the objective world.

  - **Isomorphism of Individual Perception** Between referential domains, the only available conditions for identity are those of isomorphism.

- **Chapter 3.2: Perceptual/Conceptual References** Between the perceptual domain and the conceptual domain are two primary relationships: conception and naming.

  - **3.2.1: Conception** Conception is the process of linking concepts to percepts, such that a set of percepts are identified by some concept.

    - **The Stimulus and the Response** Conditioning is a popular (extrinsic) model of conception.

    - **Neural Networks** Neural networks are a popular (intrinsic) model of conception.

  - **3.2.2: Naming** Naming is the process of denoting a concept by a percept: the percept, in virtue of this denotation, is called a symbol.

    - **Animal Cognition** Animal cognition is a part of human cognition.

    - **The Modality of Naming** Thinking can occur in any modality.

- **Chapter   3.3:   Conceptual/Conceptual   References**
Concepts can be formed recursively.

  - **3.3.1: First-Order Concepts** First-order concepts refer to percepts that refer to objects; from this reference they derive their semantic value.

  - **3.3.2: Higher-Order Concepts** Higher-order concepts refer to percepts-that-refer-to-concepts (i.e. symbols).

    - **Paradox** Concepts of concepts create the potential for both great understanding and great confusion.

Appendix B: Reference Material

B.1: Mathematical Symbols

Symbol	Interpretation
{ }	brackets used to indicate a set
=	assignment
≡	equivalence
≢	non-equivalence
≅	isomorphism
∧	conjunction (logical and)
∨	disjunction (logical or)
¬	negation (logical not)
∃	"there exists"
∀	"for every", "for all"
∪	union
∩	intersection
⊆	subset
⊇	superset
⊂	proper subset
⊃	proper superset
∈	element operator

Table B.1. Symbolic Notation

Symbol	Interpretation
O	the full set: everything
Ø	the null set: nothing
Σ	sum: summation or collection
Π	product: intersection or dichotomy
u	the physical universe
O	the subjective universe
V	the conceptual universe
Ψ	perception
Δ	communication
Φ	conception
ε	naming

B.2: Typographical Conventions

When we are talking about a thing such as an apple, it is sometimes unclear if we are referring to the physical thing (i.e. the apple object), the perceptual thing (i.e. the apple percept), or the conceptual thing (i.e. the apple concept). To disambiguate between these different uses, we adopt the following conventions:

· When we refer to the object apple, we use no typographic augmentation.

· When we refer to the perception of an apple (i.e. a percept), we use single quotes, as in 'apple'.

· When we refer to the concept of an apple, we use double quotes, as in "apple".

There are several other typographic conventions which have somewhat specific connotations in this work:

- Forward slashes are used to indicate dichotomies, as in subjective/objective.

- Hyphens are used for making compound-words.

- Emphasis is denoted *like this*.

- Hyperlinks of various kinds appear like so [http://www.CognitiveSetTheory.com].

- Glossary entries are denoted as follows: *circular reference*

B.3: Ideographic Conventions

The diagrams used in this work follow a syntax which is largely based on UML and category theory.

Things are represented as circles:

Figure B.1: Things

Relations of various kinds are depicted using lines with various arrowheads:

Relation: ─────

Parthood: ────◆

Isa: ────▷

Reference: ────→

Temporal flow: ────►

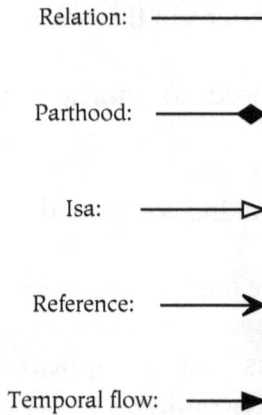

Figure B.2: Relations

Dimensions are often implicit: if a number of things are drawn immediately beneath a containing thing, then those things constitute a single dimension (which may be nominal, ordinal, interval, etc). If multiple dimensions are indicated, then they are drawn on different vertical levels. The fact that one is closer to the root indicates ontological priority: in some sense, it is more basic, and it probably evolved first (i.e. in the mind of an individual).

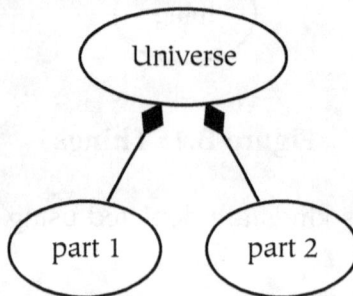

Figure B.3: Parts

Diagrams are used to express more than just part relations: they often express references between things. As an example, the following diagram expresses the following facts:

· There is a universe which is composed of two parts.

· One of those parts is a reference, and it is referring to its complement (i.e. the other part).

· The thing known as "reference-to-part" is a concept (this is indicated by the double quotes).

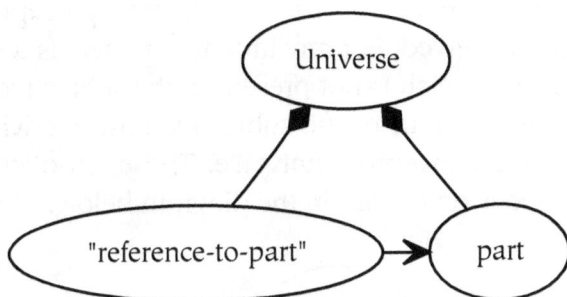

Figure B.4: References

B.4: Universes and Relations

The essence of this book can be distilled into a graph whose nodes are universes, and whose edges are specific types of referential relations. This graph is displayed below, using symbols from Section B.1, "Mathematical Symbols".

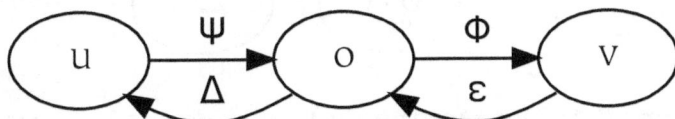

The arrows in this diagram show the typical direction of causal flow between the universes. These universes, however, also reference one another. Although there are several referential relationships between the universes, there are two which are essential: concepts reference percepts, and percepts reference objects. This is shown (without depicting the individual parts in each universe) in the diagram below:

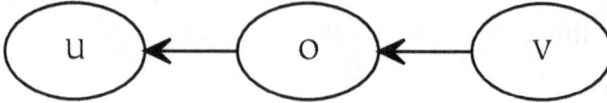

Figure B.5: The References Between the Universes

References do not map all of the world into perception: some things are not perceived. For any individual, there is a part of the physical universe which is not present in the subjective universe. Similarly, there is a part of the subjective universe which is not mapped into the conceptual universe. These left-over parts are depicted as nodes on the left in the diagram below:

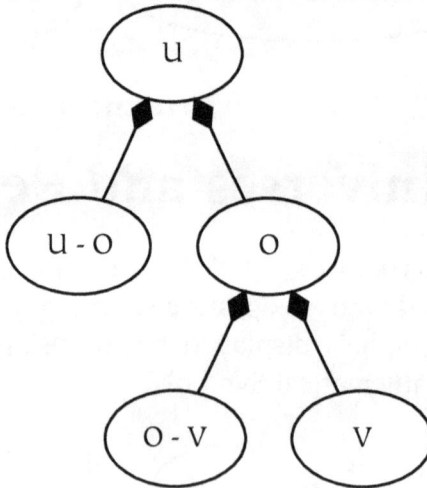

Figure B.6: The Meronomy Depicting the Universes

This diagram is a part hierarchy where the nodes are formed by dividing the parent node. We will refer to the nodes of this diagram as follows:

- U: The Physical Universe

- U-O: The Objective Domain

- O: The Subjective Universe

- O-U: The Perceptual Domain

- V: The Conceptual Universe

The nodes on the right branch of this tree contain references to the larger whole, in virtue of which they are called referential universes. Universes are formed by reference: for example, the subjective universe contains references to the physical universe, whereas the objective domain does not.

If we focus on the terminal nodes of this meronomy, we see that the universe can be composed of three distinct domains: the objective domain, the perceptual domain, and the conceptual domain. The fact that these are exclusive of one another is leveraged when the distinction is important, such as when classifying the parts of a universe. For example, when we refer to parts of the physical universe, we are often referring only to those parts which are not parts of the subjective universe: hence, they are called objects instead of percepts. The parts of the physical, subjective, and conceptual universes can be depicted as follows:

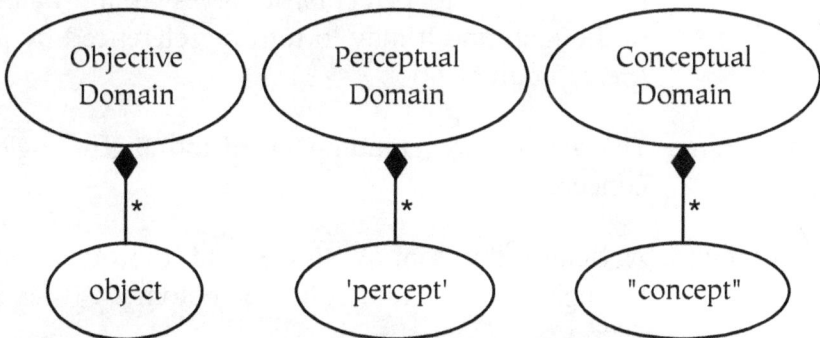

Figure B.7: The Universes

B.5: Glossary

ad infinitum   To carry on, indefinitely.

apple   If you have to ask, you will never know.

circular reference   See reference, circular.

codomain   A function maps from a domain into a codomain. For example, the sine function maps from the real numbers (its domain) into the real numbers from -1 to 1 (its image or range). However, the codomain of the sign function is also the real numbers (a superset of its image).

comparator   A comparator is a thing to which something may be compared. For example, the historical definition of a foot was the length of some individual's foot. Thus, that foot served as a comparator for all other feet.

concept   A concept is a part of the conceptual universe. It is a reference to percepts, it serves as the basis of thought, and it may in turn be referenced by a (perceptual) symbol.

conception   The act of understanding, or of forming a single concept.

dichotomy   A binary division. A single and thorough cut through an object results in a dichotomy.

dimension   That abstract quantity which is the axis of the thing being measured. It is orthogonal to the divisions which it allows. It may be nominal, ordinal, interval, or ratio.

domain   In mathematical terms, it is the set of values upon which a function may operate. It also is intended to connote the *domain of discourse*, which refers to the limitation of discourse to a particular topic.

dualism   If you believe in matter and mind as separate, then you are a dualist. En guarde!

Euclidean   A Euclidean space is one which has unit-length
space   basis vectors and which are orthogonal to each other. The familiar x,y and z axes form a three-dimensional Euclidean space: in the general case, Euclidean spaces may be of any dimensionality.

extension   The extension of a set is comprised of the elements of that set. The extension is often used to define a set: as opposed to definition in terms of properties, an extensive definition is an enumeration of all individuals possessing those properties. See also intension.

extrinsic   An extrinsic (outer) property of a thing is one which relates that thing to external things. See also intrinsic.

hierarchy   A tree-like structure which consists of one or more dimensions.

holism   Holism is the opposite of reductionism: it means that the behavior of a system cannot be determined exclusively through analysis of its parts.

hyperplane,   The prefix hyper- in these cases refers to the fact
hyperspace   that these concepts can or should be extended to an arbitrary number of dimensions. A hyperplane

is an N-dimensional plane. A hyperspace is an N-dimensional space.

intension
The intension of a set is composed of the characteristic property, or definition, of the members of that set. See also extension.

intrinsic
An intrinsic (or internal) property is one which belongs to the object itself. For example, the mass of a thing is an intrinsic property, but the weight of a thing is an extrinsic property (since it depends on gravity). See also extrinsic.

isomorphism
An isomorphism is a term which literally means "the same shape". In practice, it is a relation between two things which expresses a type of equality or congruence. For example, four points connected in a square create a structure which is isomorphic to another four points connected in a rectangle.

lexeme
A lexeme is a lexical unit, similar to a word. Although "apple" and "apples" represent different words, they are a single lexeme. Lexemes are probably closer to our underlying concepts: various words are produced by applying transformations to these lexemes as dictated by various syntactic rules.

mereology
Mereology means the study of parts. It can be seen as a complementary form of set theory which is particularly amenable to spatial representation (i.e. in terms of parts and wholes).

modality, linguistic
Modality in the linguistic sense refers to possibility. Modal logic, for example, is logic which has introduced possibility and necessity.

modality, sensory — A sensory modality most often refers to one of five types of external senses: taste, smell, touch, sight, and sound.

monism — If you believe that matter and mind are somehow one and the same, then you are a monist. If you further believe that only matter is real, you are a materialist. If you instead believe that only mind is real, you are a materialist.

morpheme — A morpheme is a phoneme which has an associated meaning.

N-space — N-space is a space which consists of N-dimensions (or perhaps more precisely, is of rank N). For example, physical space is a kind of 3-space, and spacetime is a kind of 4-space.

natural kind — A natural kind is an object which *truly exists*. This means roughly that the object is *more valid* than an object composed of a part of that object in conjunction with another object (the latter composite, in that case, would not be a natural kind). The front half of a turkey and the back half of a trout, for example, would not be an obvious choice for a natural kind.

nominalism — A belief that the objects in the world are objects in virtue of only their names. In other words, there are no privileged objects or natural kinds: how we conceptually divide the universe is up to us.

object — A physical thing, which may be of high dimensionality (i.e. it is understood to contain temporal and perhaps other parts).

ontology — Ontology literally means the study of being, or existence. For example, a word may also have ontological validity (it is valid as a reference) if it exists as a concept.

ontological priority	A thing which occurs ontologically prior to another thing comes before that thing. For example, if a thing is a concept which is used in the definition of a subsequent thing, then the former thing is (necessarily) ontologically prior.
orthogonal	Orthogonal means perpendicular. In two dimensions, orthogonal vectors (lines) form a right angle to one another.
part	A part is a thing which is contained in another thing, and is smaller than that containing thing (in virtue of which it is technically called a *proper part*).
partition	A partition of a thing is a complete or exhaustive decomposition of that thing into parts. Every bit of the whole is contained in some part, and no bit of a part is contained in more than one part.
percept	A subjective referent to a thing (either an object or a concept).
perception	The act of experiencing reality or some part thereof: the witnessing of a percept.
phoneme	A part of a spoken word, such as a syllable.
proper part	A thing which is contained in another thing, and is necessarily smaller than that other thing.
range	The range (or image) of a function consists of all of the values which might be a result of the application of that function. See also domain, codomain.

reductionism   The thesis of reductionism is that the behavior of a system cannot be determined exclusively through analysis of its parts. See also holism.

reference   A reference is a representation of a thing, as opposed to the thing itself.

reference, circular   See circular reference.

relation   A relation is a definition which is established between multiple things.

semantics   The meaning of words. See also syntax.

set   A collection of things which is treated as a singular entity. See also concept.

signified   Saussure's term for a thought or idea, for which we use the term *concept*.

signifier   Saussure's term for a percept that corresponds to a concept, which we refer to as a symbol.

symbol   A percept which references (represents, denotes) a concept. This is enabled by the act of naming. (the rules by which the semantics of words may be combined)

syntax   The rules by which the semantics of words may be combined. See also semantics.

taxonomy   A taxonomy is a hierarchy of kinds or types.

universe   A universe is a set of things which is a complete whole. It is either the physical universe, or some set of references to it.

Appendix C: Bibliography

Where would we be without large collections of non-randomly arraged symbols? Not your local library.

[Langer] *An introduction to symbolic logic*. Susanne Katherina Knauth Langer. ISBN: 0486601641.

[Chomsky] *Aspects of the theory of syntax*. Noam Chomsky. ISBN: 0262530074.

[Bernays] *Axiomatic set theory*. Paul Bernays. ISBN: 0486666379.

[Suppes] *Axiomatic set theory*. Patrick Suppes. ISBN: 0486616304.

[Lévy] *Basic set theory*. Azriel Lévy. ISBN: 0486420795.

[Shantideva] *Bodhicaryavatara*. Shantideva, Vesna A. Wallace, B. Alan Wallace. ISBN: 1559390611.

[Lawvere] *Conceptual mathematics: a first introduction to categories*. F. W. Lawvere, Stephen Hoel Schanuel. ISBN: 0521478170.

[Gardenfors] *Conceptual spaces: the geometry of thought*. Peter Gärdenfors. ISBN: 0262572192.

[Stjernfelt] *Diagrammatology: an investigation on the borderlines of phenomenology, ontology, and semiotics*. Frederik Stjernfelt. ISBN: 1402056516.

[Hein] *Discrete Structures, Logic, and Computability*. James L. Hein. ISBN: 0763772062.

266

[Domjan] *Domjan and Burkhard's The principles of learning and behavior.* Michael Domjan, Barbara Burkhard. ISBN: 0534189121.

[Jackendoff] *Foundations of language: brain, meaning, grammar, evolution.* Ray Jackendoff. ISBN: 0199264376.

[Quine] *From a logical point of view: 9 logico-philosophical essays.* Willard Van Orman Quine. ISBN: 0674323513.

[Yen] *Fuzzy logic: intelligence, control, and information.* John Yen, Reza Langari. ISBN: 0135258170.

[Rucker] *Infinity and the Mind.* Rudy Rucker. ISBN: 0553255312.

[Levine] *Introduction to neural and cognitive modeling.* Daniel S. Levine. ISBN: 0805820051.

[Jackendoff] *Language, consciousness, culture: essays on mental structure.* Ray Jackendoff. ISBN: 026210119X.

[Lyons] *Language and linguistics.* John Lyons. ISBN: 0521297753.

[Schwartz] *Learning and memory.* Barry Schwartz, Daniel Reisberg. ISBN: 0393959112.

[Cruse] *Lexical semantics.* D. A. Cruse. ISBN: 0521276438.

[Allwein] *Logical reasoning with diagrams.* Gerard Allwein, Jon Barwise. ISBN: 0195104277.

[Bunt] *Mass Terms and Model-Theoretic Semantics.* Harry C. Bunt. ISBN: 0521105919.

[Churchland] *Matter and consciousness: a contemporary introduction to the philosophy of mind.* Paul M. Churchland. ISBN: 0262530740.

[Lycan] *Mind and cognition: a reader.* William G. Lycan. ISBN: 0631167633.

[Grossberg] *Neural networks and natural intelligence.* Stephen Grossberg. ISBN: 026207107X.

[Quine] *Ontological relativity and other essays.* W. V. Quine, Willard Van Orman Quine. ISBN: 0231083572.

[Simons] *Parts: a study in ontology.* Peter Simons. ISBN: 0199241465.

[Moltmann] *Parts and Wholes in Semantics.* Friederike Moltmann. ISBN: 0195154932.

[Lewis] *Parts of classes.* David K. Lewis. ISBN: 063117656X.

[Jackendoff] *Patterns in the mind: language and human nature.* Ray Jackendoff. ISBN: 0465054625.

[Gyamtso] *Progressive stages of meditation on emptiness.* Tsultrim Gyamtso. ISBN: 0951147706.

[Block] *Readings in philosophy of psychology.* Ned Joel Block. ISBN: 067474876X.

[Chomsky] *Rules and representations.* Noam Chomsky. ISBN: 0231048270.

[Potter] *Set theory and its philosophy: a critical introduction.* Michael D. Potter. ISBN: 0199270414.

[Stoll] *Set theory and logic.* Robert Roth Stoll. ISBN: 0486638294.

[Brown] *Syntax: a linguistic introduction to sentence structure.* E. K. Brown, J. E. Miller. ISBN: 0044455615.

[Murphy] *The big book of concepts.* Gregory L. Murphy. ISBN: 0262632993.

[Varela] *The embodied mind : cognitive science and human experience.* Francisco J., Varela, Evan Thompson, Eleanor Rosch. ISBN: 0262720213.

[Minsky] *The emotion machine: commensense thinking, artificial intelligence, and the future of the human mind.* Marvin Lee Minsky. ISBN: 0743276639.

[Devlin] *The joy of sets: fundamentals of contemporary set theory.* Keith J. Devlin. ISBN: 0387940944.

[Boole] *The laws of thought.* George Boole. ISBN: 1591020891.

[Percy] *The message in the bottle: how queer man is, how queer language is, and what one has to do with the other.* Walker Percy. ISBN: 0312254016.

[Hofstadter] *The mind's I: fantasies and reflections on self and soul.* Douglas R. Hofstadter, Daniel Clement Dennett. ISBN: 0553345842.

[Gallistel] *The organization of learning.* Charles R. Gallistel. ISBN: 026257098X.

[Tiles] *The philosophy of set theory: an historical introduction to Cantor's paradise.* Mary Tiles. ISBN: 0486435202.

[Barron] *The precious treasury of the basic space of phenomena.* Longchenpa, Richard Barron, Susanne Fairclough. ISBN: 1881847322.

[Minsky] *The society of mind.* Marvin Minsky. ISBN: 0671657135.

[Pinker] *The stuff of thought: language as a window into human nature.* Steven Pinker. ISBN: 0670063274.

[McCreight] *The syntax of objects.* Tim McCreight. ISBN: 1929565135.

[Capra] *The Tao of physics: an exploration of the parallels between modern physics and Eastern mysticism.* Fritjof Capra. ISBN: 0877735948.

[Maturana] *The tree of knowledge: the biological roots of human understanding.* Humberto R. Maturana, Francisco J. Varela. ISBN: 0877736421.

[Armstrong] *Universals: an opinionated introduction.* David Malet Armstrong. ISBN: 0813307724.

[Gersho] *Vector quantization and signal compression.* Allen Gersho, Robert M. Gray. ISBN: 0792391810.

[Braitenberg] *Vehicles: experiments in synthetic psychology.* Valentino Braitenberg. ISBN: 0262521121.

[Kosslyn] *Wet mind: the new cognitive neuroscience.* Stephen Michael Kosslyn, Olivier Koenig. ISBN: 002917595X.

[Lakoff] *Where mathematics comes from: how the embodied mind brings mathematics into being.* George Lakoff, Rafael E. Núñez. ISBN: 0465037712.

[Bohm] *Wholeness and the implicate order.* David Bohm. ISBN: 0415289793.

[Quine] *Word and object.* Willard Van Orman Quine. ISBN: 0262670011.

[Pinker] *Words and rules: the ingredients of language.* Steven Pinker. ISBN: 0060958405.

[Austin] *Zen and the brain: toward an understanding of meditation and consciousness.* James H. Austin. ISBN: 0262511096.

www.ingramcontent.com/pod-product-compliance
Lightning Source LLC
Chambersburg PA
CBHW031502270326
41930CB00006B/211